TEACHING ORIENTEERING

SECOND EDITION

Carol McNeill

Jean Cory-Wright

Tom Renfrew

Published in collaboration with the British Orienteering Federation

HARVEYS

HUMAN
KINETICS

British Library Cataloguing-in-Publication Data

A catalogue record for this book is available from the British Library.

ISBN   185137 0250 (Harveys)

Library of Congress Cataloging-in-Publication Data

McNeill, Carol
   Teaching orienteering / Carol McNeill, Jean Cory-Wright, Tom Renfrew. --2nd edition.
      p. cm.
   "Published in collaboration with the British Orienteering Federation."
   ISBN 0-88011-804-0
   1. Orienteering--Study and teaching. I. Cory-Wright, Jean. II. Renfrew, Tom. III. British Orienteering Federation. IV. Title.
   GV200.4.M45 1997
   796.58'07--dc21
                                                                97-17531
                                                                CIP

ISBN   0-88011-804-0 (Human Kinetics)

Photographer (cover): Jonathon Taylor
Cover Designer: Stuart Cartwright
Printer: Paramount Printing
Printed in Hong Kong

10 9 8 7 6 5 4 3 2 1

HARVEYS

12-16 Main Street
Doune, Perthshire FK16 6BJ, United Kingdom
44-1786-841202

HUMAN KINETICS

Web site: http://www.humankinetics.com/

United States: Human Kinetics
PO Box 5076, Champaign, IL 61825-5076
1-800-747-4457
e-mail: humank@hkusa.com

Canada: Human Kinetics
Box 24040, Windsor, ON N8Y 4Y9
1-800-465-7301 (in Canada only)
e-mail: humank@hkcanada.com

Europe: Human Kinetics
PO Box IW14, Leeds, LS16 6TR, United Kingdom
(44) 1132 781708
e-mail: humank@hkeurope.com

Australia: Human Kinetics
57A Price Avenue, Lower Mitcham, South Australia 5062
(088) 277 1555
e-mail: humank@hkaustralia.com

New Zealand: Human Kinetics
PO Box 105-231, Auckland 1
(09) 523 3462
e-mail: humank@hknewz.com

Contents

Preface

Orienteering is a sport and recreational activity which can be pursued at many levels, and appeals to both genders and all ages; it is an exciting way of learning the skills needed to navigate through unfamiliar but well-charted country. It can begin with 8-year-olds learning basic ideas in the classroom, school grounds or local parks, and can be developed to become a challenging outdoor pursuit for all.

The educational value provided by orienteering's blend of navigational and physical skills has long been recognised, giving it a permanent place in the primary and secondary school core curriculum in the UK. Through schools' leagues, membership of local orienteering clubs and - at the peak of success - area or national representation, youngsters can pursue orienteering as a competitive sport on a regular basis; schools can aim for area or national titles in the annual schools' championship.

Permanent orienteering courses are established in parks and woods, and on open heath and moorland, in many parts of Britain; they provide a ready-made base for most of the outdoor exercises in these pages.

This book provides complete teaching schemes and a multitude of lessons, games and training activities for primary and secondary pupils, all requiring the minimum of specialist equipment or clothing. The aims of each exercise, the age group and the skill levels are clearly stated and supplementary exercises suggested. The teacher will always want to plan each activity session in such a way that the children taking part feel happy and safe; a lost and frightened or exhausted youngster is usually lost to orienteering for ever. When well taught - following the sequences and ideas developed in this book - orienteering takes its place as one of the most exciting and satisfying of outdoor pursuits.

Teaching Orienteering - written by three experts in their field - can fairly claim to be the standard work on the subject and deserves a place as a teachers' resource in all schools and outdoor centres.

Clive Allen

Note: Clive Allen is a former chairman of the British Orienteering Federation and member of the Development and Promotion Committee of the International Orienteering Federation

About the authors

Carol McNeill MBE, Dip Ed; Sports Coaching Diploma; British Orienteering Federation Senior Coach. Carol has had over 20 years experience of teaching and coaching orienteering to children and adults of all ages. She has had a particular interest in developing orienteering in schools. She has represented Britain in 7 World Orienteering Championships gaining 7th place in Finland in 1979. In 1986 and 1994 she won gold medals in her age class at the Veteran World Cup.

Jean Cory-Wright BSc, Dip Ed; British Orienteering Federation Coach. Jean is currently at the Auckland Institute of Technology in New Zealand (outdoor leadership course). She has over 12 years teaching experience with the Ardentinny Outdoor Education Centre, John Ruskin School, Cumbria Schools Outdoor Education Service, Charlotte Mason College for Outdoor Education. She has represented Britain in 6 World Orienteering Championships.

Tom Renfrew ADPE, BA, MSc is a senior lecturer at the University of Strathclyde. He is director of the BA Degree Programmes Sport and Outdoor Education in the community. A qualified coach who has chaired the British Orienteering Federation Coaching Committee, Tom has written a number of books on the sport and is currently researching ways in which persons with learning difficulties can be integrated into the mainstream of the sport.

Acknowledgements

Terry Foxton (maps); Barry Pope, David Briggs, Jonathon Taylor, Rod Organ, Anne Braggins, Glynn Roberts, Clive Allen (photographs); Harvey Map Services Ltd (maps); Peter Palmer; Jack Ramsden; Ardentinny Centre staff; Lindy McConnel; Cherry Simpson; Colin Henderson; Tony Thornley; Sue Kysow WCOC; Calvert Trust; Silva UK Ltd; British Orienteering Federation; Scottish Orienteering Association; South East Orienteering Association; West Midlands Orienteering Association; London Orienteering Klub; Clydeside Orienteers; Octavian Droobers; Dudley Metropolitan Borough; Birmingham City Leisure; Central Regional Council; Forth Valley Orienteers; Moravian Orienteering Club; Walton Chasers; Children of Penny Bridge and Satterthwaite Primary Schools.

Introduction

This book is written as a key reference to the sport of orienteering for teachers, leaders or coaches. It provides a 'how to' approach to introducing and developing the skills and techniques of the sport.

Each suggested exercise is self contained and has been laid out to allow the teacher to quickly determine the aim of the exercise, the age group it is suitable for, the time the exercise will take to complete and the equipment needed. This extensive collection of ideas and strategies can be dipped into time and again by busy teachers to satisfy particular requirements.

For relative newcomers to the sport, chapter 1 provides guidelines for the design of orienteering programmes and schemes of work, the foundation for individual lessons. Teachers wishing to plan a complete programme should start here.

Chapter 11 expands the guidelines to bring them into line with current UK practice in primary and secondary schools and in further education.

Compass use is placed relatively late in the book suggesting that although a valuable aid to navigation it is not a substitute for acquiring sound map skills.

The order of the early chapters (2, 3 and 4) follows a logical progression, the authors recommending that beginners commence the sport in familiar easy terrain (classroom or school/centre grounds) before moving into parks and woodland. In these chapters some exercises have similar titles (score orienteering appears three times, for example) but in each case the exercise is planned for the relevant environment.

The book is not intended to provide a page-by-page sequence of lessons. Programmes may take lessons from various chapters, not necessarily in the same order as the book. It is a compilation of exercises and activities grouped under broad headings from which the teacher can select the most suitable for the particular course.

The authors believe that Teaching Orienteering is a reference book that will be used over and over again by anyone who teaches orienteering or navigation.

The second edition of the book retains the tried and tested, and well received, format of the original edition but the material has been extensively updated and extended.

EQUIPMENT REQUIRED FOR LESSONS
The equipment required for each lesson is indicated by a dot above the appropriate symbol at the top right of each lesson page:

KEY TO SYMBOLS

	Control MARKERS to hang at control sites
	MINI MARKERS for classroom or playground
	MAPS
	CLOCK
	COMPASSES
Ĕ	Control CODES to identify control sites
	Control PUNCHES to mark control cards
CC	Control CARDS to punch at controls
CD	Control DESCRIPTION LISTS
	PENCILS
	PAPER

1

TEACHING ORIENTEERING

WHAT IS ORIENTEERING

Orienteering is an outdoor sport which usually takes place in woodland or forest. However local parks, campuses and even school grounds provide excellent opportunities for introductory exercises and small events.

Orienteering is a navigation sport using specially drawn and detailed maps.

An orienteering course consists of a series of control points which have to be visited in order, in the shortest possible time.

The control points are distinctive features marked on the map by circles. The sites are marked on the ground by large orange and white 'kites' hung clearly at the feature circled on the map.

Each control has a code number for identification and a punch with a unique pin pattern. This punch is used to mark a control card to prove that the correct control has been visited.

A competitor carries the map, a control description/code list and a control card.

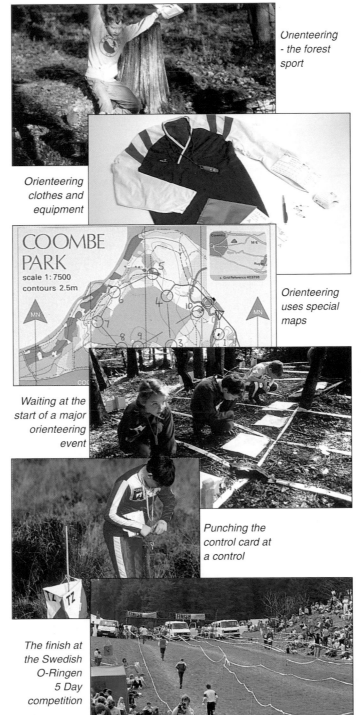

Orienteering - the forest sport

Orienteering clothes and equipment

Orienteering uses special maps

Waiting at the start of a major orienteering event

Punching the control card at a control

The finish at the Swedish O-Ringen 5 Day competition

The control card is used to record start and finish times. A control description list gives the code and the control feature as an aid to navigation.

All the competitor then needs is a whistle for safety, a plastic map case to protect the map and a compass to keep the map set to north.

At an event participants choose the course suitable for their age and experience. People of all ages can take part, walking or running.

Starting at minute intervals, competitors first copy the course on to their own map from the 'master map', then they are off to find the controls in the right order.

As a competitor, the aim is to find the controls as quickly as possible. The choice of route between controls is theirs. The winner is the one who completes the course in the fastest time.

Orienteering is an individual sport demanding continuous concentration to keep to the chosen route.

VALUE OF ORIENTEERING

The sport has much to offer young people. Increasingly it has a justified place in the curriculum of primary and secondary schools. Some of the claims made for the sport are identified below.

Conceptual aspects

• The sport is basically concerned with navigation. This involves making decisions about map interpretation, taking and using compass bearings.

• It demands that competitors constantly interpret information, usually from map to ground.

• It encourages youngsters to classify and analyse land patterns and familiarises them with land use maps.

• It lends itself to working across the curriculum. Chapter 11 expands on this idea.

Physical aspects

• Orienteering is a running sport. Cardiovascular endurance and general fitness are healthy by-products of moving through varied terrain at speed.

• Speed, agility and strength are required to compete successfully. Exercises for improvement of these components are presented in Chapter 10.

• A major feature of the sport is the mixture of mental and physical challenge involved. Youngsters often train harder and run further when they have the added interest of map reading.

Social and personal aspects

The social and personal values of all activities, ranging from competitive sport or recreation to intense adventure activity have long been recognised as a valuable contribution to personal development. Orienteering has much to contribute.

• Orienteering fosters self reliance and confidence. Children have the responsibility for making their own decisions. Finding controls in a forest through successful map reading leaves children with a genuine sense of achievement.

• Youngsters often start the sport working in groups and have to learn to work with one another.

• Opportunities are presented in an outdoor environment for pupil-teacher relationships to be improved.

• Young people respond to physical demands made on their bodies. Few orienteers smoke.

• Young orienteers are encouraged to have clear aims and aspirations, to be methodical, to work hard and constructively in achieving them.

• The sport provides opportunities for children, often from cities and towns, to travel to a variety of stimulating rural settings. It encourages an awareness and appreciation of the environment and the need to observe the country code.

• The sport has an appeal to family groups. Its structure allows parents and children to compete at their own level at the same event.

Many outdoor activities are costly and have a danger element that necessitates a low pupil-teacher ratio. Orienteering has the advantage of being a relatively inexpensive sport requiring very little specialist equipment. Safety procedures are well established and the forest is usually a relatively sheltered environment in poor weather conditions.

Most countries have suitable orienteering terrain; in the major cities parks are often used and the school setting is an ideal starting point for introducing and developing orienteering techniques.

AIMS AND OBJECTIVES

Identify the group you are working with and establish aims and objectives according to their age.

Age 7-10 years

Age 9-12 years

Ages 13-15, 16-17, adults

Within the tables on this page and the next will be found a list of maps suitable for each age group, followed by a list of skills to be taught; these skills are listed in an order recommended within national coaching schemes and can be used as a progress checklist for teacher or pupil. Teaching methods, physical aspects and evaluation give ideas for variety as well as for making the scheme of work complete and effective.

Whichever group you have, before you can start teaching them to orienteer, they must understand two fundamental concepts:

- that the map is a picture of the ground.
- that the map must be held so that it corresponds directly with the surrounding ground, i.e. it is orientated or 'set'.

With children under 10 years of age time must be spent establishing these concepts before further progress can be made. The classroom lessons (p15-18), picture maps (p25), string orienteering (p31,38) and understanding maps (p19) are examples of lessons which can be used.

To maximise the learning process every lesson should include a review of what has been covered - and learnt. This review should be summarised again, ideally the following day or at the beginning of the next lesson.

EVALUATE ON A REGULAR BASIS

The teacher or coach should continually evaluate his/her own effectiveness by asking:

'What did they do?'

'What did they learn?'

'Was it worthwhile?'

'What is the next step?'

'Are they working at the right level?'

'Are any children in need of special help?'

Age Group: 7-10 years

Aims
- *to create an interest in the sport of orienteering*
- *to develop an understanding of the map as a picture of the ground*

MAPS
- desk maps
- classroom/hall maps
- playground (large scale) and picture maps
- park (1:5000, 1:10000) maps

SKILLS - what to teach
- plans, shapes - map as a picture
- colours, line features, buildings
- orientation (setting) of map to terrain
- following easy line features - paths, tracks, progressing to streams, walls, fences, fields
- no route choice - controls on line features initially, at every decision point
- map contact - folding, thumbing
- control points - punching, codes
- control card and control descriptions

TEACHING METHODS
- map walks with instructor
- streamer course
- string courses, picture maps, direct method
- white - easy yellow standard courses (controls at every decision point), in pairs or as individual
- point to point and score orienteering
- star exercises

EVALUATION
Games, worksheets, successful completion of orienteering courses

Age Group: 9-12 years

Aims
- *to develop an interest in orienteering*
- *to develop map reading skills as an aid to navigation*
- *to introduce the forest as one of several outdoor environments*
- *to develop self-confidence through successful decision-making*

MAPS
- classroom, hall maps
- playground, centre, camp maps
- park map
- woodland (1:5000, 1:10000) maps

SKILLS
- map legend and scale
- orientation of map to terrain, introduce the map-guide compass
- following line features, use as handrails
- recognition of features beside lines, e.g. crags, boulders, buildings
- one obvious route, short cuts to path routes
- introduction to contours (hills, steep/flat)
- map contact - folding, thumbing
- organisation of control card and descriptions

TEACHING METHODS
- white - yellow courses, plenty of controls, on line features
- in pairs or as individuals
- point to point, score and line orienteering, star exercises
- badge incentive scheme

PHYSICAL ASPECTS
- fun runs, games, circuits, relays with map

EVALUATION
- games, worksheets, successful completion of orienteering courses

Age 13-15, 16-17 years and adults

Aims
- *to navigate through the terrain with the aid of map and compass*

MAPS
- classroom/hall maps
- playground, centre, camp maps
- park (1:5000, 1:10000) maps
- woodland, forest (1:10000, 1:15000) maps
- mountain maps (1:25000, 1:40000, 1:50000)

SKILLS - INTRODUCTION (A)
- map legend, scale
- orientation of map to terrain
- use of line features as handrails
- simple route choice
- rough orienteering - long legs with good catching features
- fine orienteering - short legs of detailed map reading
- use of attack points, aiming off with compass
- basic use of compass/thumb compass
- distance judgement
- development of basic contour appreciation

TEACHING METHODS (A)
- yellow - orange - red courses, as individuals
- colour coded courses

EVALUATION (A)
- games, puzzle-O, worksheets, quizzes, colour coded badge scheme

SKILLS - DEVELOPMENT (B)
(see coaching handbook)
- building of contour perception into navigational techniques
- orienteer along large hills, distinct marshes, clearings, thickets; use of vegetation changes
- read contours in detail
- further use of compass and pacing
- simplification of routes
- race preparation and event analysis

TEACHING METHODS (B)
- green - blue standard courses
- self-programmed project (see 16+ modules)
- lessons and exercises in 'technique training'
- badge incentive schemes

PHYSICAL ASPECTS (B)
- training for orienteering as a running sport
- warming up and stretching (especially adults)

EVALUATION (B)
- progress through colour coded courses

ORIENTEERING SKILLS STEP BY STEP

To achieve the aims and objectives, in the following pages this book outlines sample schemes of work for different age groups.

The schemes of work are a guide to the teaching of the skills needed for successful orienteering. These skills can be summarised as follows:

Understanding of map symbols

Recognising map features on the ground

Orientating the map

Following handrails

Relocation

Route choice

Use of the compass

Simplification of navigational problems

The fundamental skill in orienteering is orientating the map (also called setting the map). The key to moving with a map is

- recognising the pattern of features on the ground as being the same as the pattern on the map, and
- always holding the map so that you are looking along the route to be followed, with the map matching the ground

The map can be orientated either by setting to features on the ground or by using a compass. To set to features on the ground the map must be turned until the pattern of features on the ground matches those on the map. To set by the compass the map must be turned until map north matches compass (magnetic) north.

Orientating the map is a thread which runs through the lessons that follow.

THE STEP SYSTEM: PROGRESSION OF ORIENTEERING SKILLS

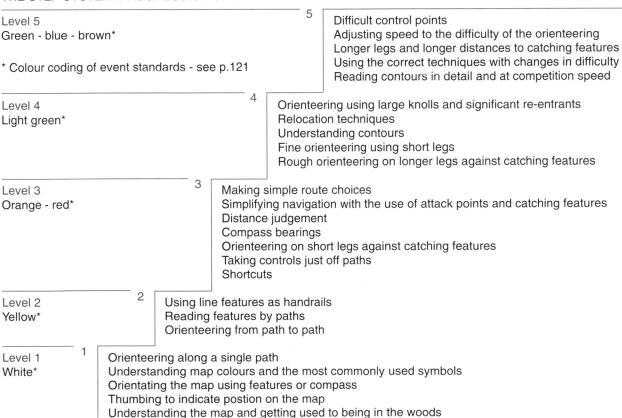

Level 5
Green - blue - brown*

* Colour coding of event standards - see p.121

5
Difficult control points
Adjusting speed to the difficulty of the orienteering
Longer legs and longer distances to catching features
Using the correct techniques with changes in difficulty
Reading contours in detail and at competition speed

Level 4
Light green*

4
Orienteering using large knolls and significant re-entrants
Relocation techniques
Understanding contours
Fine orienteering using short legs
Rough orienteering on longer legs against catching features

Level 3
Orange - red*

3
Making simple route choices
Simplifying navigation with the use of attack points and catching features
Distance judgement
Compass bearings
Orienteering on short legs against catching features
Taking controls just off paths
Shortcuts

Level 2
Yellow*

2
Using line features as handrails
Reading features by paths
Orienteering from path to path

Level 1
White*

1
Orienteering along a single path
Understanding map colours and the most commonly used symbols
Orientating the map using features or compass
Thumbing to indicate position on the map
Understanding the map and getting used to being in the woods

SCHEMES OF WORK

Having established the objectives, the next stage is designing a programme or scheme of work. Secondary school teachers and others interested in a modular approach should refer to the chapter 'Orienteering Programmes in Education' which gives guidelines for modular courses. The sample schemes in this section should serve as a useful guide for those for whom they are appropriate. In adapting them some of the following questions should be asked:

How long is each session and how many sessions are there?

Do you have a school or centre base for introductory and theory lessons?

Is there access to a park or woodland with an orienteering map?

How does travel affect the length of teaching time?

Will you teach any theory, cover it in handouts or leave it to the students to pursue themselves?

Will you introduce one of the incentive badge schemes (p149), and how will you assess progress?

Schemes of work

1 Primary 7-10 years

2 Secondary 12-14 years

3 Secondary 12-17 years

4 Outdoor centre or youth camp

5 Orienteering club, youth club or youth organisation (e.g. scouts)

6 Adults - further education class

7 Other groups: Police and armed forces
Disabled persons
Parents

Preparation is essential in this sport. Do not be tempted to initiate a scheme of work until everything is ready. Follow the instructions in 'Practical Preparations' (p12) and buy a Harvey Starter Pack (see p153).

Be prepared to adapt the programme to the progress of the group remembering that lots of repetition is necessary for sound learning. Plan exercises so that the least able can find all the controls or select lessons for mixed ability groups such as star exercises (p27,36,42), score orienteering (p17,24,30,37) or pairs orienteering (p48).

SCHEME 1   **School children, age 7-10 years**

8 lessons of 40-60 minutes
(Classroom or playground maps)

1 Introductory lesson - classroom (p15)

2 Point to point orienteering - classroom (p16)

3 Star exercise - playground (p27)

4 Point to point orienteering - playground (p28)

5 Score orienteering - playground (p24)

6 Point to point relay orienteering - playground (p28)

7 Line orienteering - classroom/hall, playground (p18,31)

8 Introduction to local park: direct method (p39) or star exercises plus point to point course (p35,36).

SCHEME 2   **School children, age 12-14 years**

8 lessons of 60-70 minutes
(No park or woodland immediately accessible)

1 Classroom introduction (p13,15), playground star (p27) - assess ability, potential and interest

2 *Practical:* playground score (p24) or 5 point to point courses (p28)

   Theory: o-maps, legend identification, controls, route choice, discussion - card games, bingo (p95,98,106)

3 *Practical:* playground 3-man relay (p28,47)

   Theory: memory games (p97), setting the map (p85,16) - use map and course for lesson 4

4* Park or forest permanent course (p35,36)

5 *Theory:* introduction to compass (p71,72)

   Practical: playground compass exercise (p75,76)

6* Park or forest map walk, map setting with compass Two short point to point courses from same start (i) very easy (ii) easy - line features, route choice (p132)

7 Preparation for lesson 8. Going to an event (p50), master maps (p21), punching relay (p118), games (p95,98,99,102,106)

8* Local club competition - easiest course Project 3 - log book and course analysis (p126)

* These visits or a programme of local competitions are necessary to run a satisfactory scheme of work for this age group

Further work
Refer to skills progression (p7) and 'further work' sections of lessons. Use team games, relays, puzzle 'o' and other games to maintain interest. Carefully plan visits to woodland to maximise time, e.g. star exercises or 2-3 short (1km) skill-based courses.

SCHEME 3   School children, age 12-17 years

Lessons 90 - 120 minutes

(Park, woodland or permanent courses accessible)

1 School:
Introduction, what is orienteering (p3,13,15)

2 Park:
Map walk, star exercise, point to point course (p36)
<u>or</u>
Permanent course - map walk and course (p51)

3 School:
Theory: setting and thumbing the map (p85), classroom score (p17), playground relay (p28) or score (p24), games e.g. feature identification (p95,98,99,106)

4 Park or woodland:
Using compass needle to set the map (p85) - practice on walk and put controls out for relay, route choice in pairs (p41), 2-person relay, very short 0.5-0.8km (p47)

5 School:
Video or film (p13,153)
Theory: handrails and collecting features (p86,88)
<u>either</u>
contours (p49,91), drawing profiles (p104, also 97,95,107)
<u>or</u>
compass (p71), using compass to cut corners (p73), bearing/distance measurement (p82), running game, e.g. punching (p118) or mini map races (p33)

6 Park or woodland:
Contours introduction (p49)
<u>or</u>
Compass practice (p72,73,77,78,79)
Point to point course - line features, route choice

7 School:
Event procedures and preparation (p50), master maps (p21)

8 Local club competition

Without permanent controls the practical sessions are organised more easily with two staff members. One sets off to put out controls 5 minutes ahead of the group. The other teacher or nominated student starts individuals off at 2 minute intervals. A worksheet (p106,107) or word search (p105) can be answered in the waiting periods.

Further work

Refer to skills progressions and 'further work' sections of lessons.

SCHEME 4   Outdoor centre - youth camp

Half-day sessions

1 Introductory session, visual presentation (p13), map walk, score orienteering (p37) *45-60 minutes
- could be done one evening*

2 Map walk, star exercise and point to point orienteering in woodland (p36) *90-120 minutes*
<u>or</u> permanent course, map walk and point to point course (p51) *90-120 minutes*

3 Yellow standard point to point competition (p29,132)

Extra orienteering sessions could include:
- introduction to night orienteering (p52)
- puzzle orienteering (p62)
- Norwegian event (p57)
- compass sessions (chapter 6)

Also games section (chapter 8) and alternative orienteering (chapter 9), e.g. mountain, bike or canoe orienteering.

SCHEME 5 Orienteering club, youth organisation - beginners

90-120 minute sessions
Woodland

1 • Map walk, taped line, controls (p35)
 • Punching game with fixed control card (p118)
  - organisation of control card and descriptions
 • White standard point to point course - running and punching, repeat (time second circuit only) (p132)

2 • String course in pairs, 2 loops 250-400 metres (p38)
 • Star exercise with singles and mini courses (p36,42)
 • Pace count double-paces round one of the string loops - record results and keep for session 4 (p45)
 • Card games and memory tests (p95,97)

3 • Route choice in pairs of fours (p41)
 • Map setting with compass (p71,72)
 • Team score event (p43)

4 • Distance estimation (p44) and pacing (p45)
 • Line orienteering, requiring simple distance estimation skills (p40)
 • 2 person relay (p28,47)

5 • Introduction to contours (p49)
 • Relocation for beginners (p46)
 • Puzzle orienteering (p62)

6 Use of compass exercises (after theory, chapter 6)

Indoor sessions
 • Videos (p13,153)
 • Master map copying (p21)
 • Handrails and collecting features (p86,88)
 • Use of compass (p74)
 • Event analysis (p126)
 • Recommended reading (p153)

Notes
Keep all exercises under 2km. Write out and copy the programme of exercises for each session. Explain the aims of each exercise. Attach a more experienced club member to each beginner. Invite everyone to help with the organisation of your next event.

SCHEME 6 Adults - further education class

6 weeks (16 hours)
This course should preceed or coincide with a series of local events. An assistant to hang controls will ease the organisation.

1 Indoors:
 Jigsaw mixer (p94), classroom team score (p17), video/visual introduction to orienteering (p13), look at orienteering maps - legend etc, setting and thumbing the map (p85), legend memory game (p97), training video (p153)

2 Park/permanent course
 Star exercise (p36), short (1-2km) point to point course - include organisation of control card and descriptions (p50)

 Theory: compass introduction (p71,72,85)

3 Park/woodland
 Using the compass - orientation and cutting corners (p72,73,77)

 Theory: compass bearings (p74), attack points (p87), aiming off (p89), bearing/distance measurement game (p102)

4 Park/forest
 Compass bearings, 3 courses with common starts, e.g. rough compass/aiming off (p79), attack points (p42), control picking (p80)

 Theory: route choice/collecting features (p88), traffic lights (p58), training video (p153)

5 Park/forest
 Introduction to contours (p49), distance estimation (p44), team score (p43)

 Theory: contour revision - drawing profiles (p104,107)

6 Park/forest
 Pacing (p45), compass and pacing (p82), surprise map drawing (p67)

 Theory: course planning (p101,131)

7 Park/forest
 Relocation (p46), self perpetuating course - easy control sites (p66)

 Theory: the competition (p50), master maps (p21), event analysis (p126), physical/mental fitness (ch10)

8 Competition
 2 courses (i) medium (orange) (ii) short hard (green) - everyone does both courses (p132)

 Theory: debrief, local club information

Notes
The theory can be given out as notes or used for bad weather days. Adapt to suit circumstances.

7 OTHER GROUPS

Police and armed forces

The ability to read maps is an integral part of cadet and officer training. Orienteering offers an ideal activity for learning navigational skills as well as being a useful tool for developing decision-making and other leadership skills.

Efficient search-and-rescue also demands a competent understanding of maps especially in wooded terrain where micro searching is often necessary. Copies of local orienteering maps should be held by the police to aid their organisation of such searches.

Disabled persons

Selecting and adapting lessons for people with physical disabilities or who have learning difficulties must be done with careful consideration given to the specific disability.

Persons who have partial sight and those in wheelchairs are naturally restricted to suitable terrain. Parkland, campus areas and playgrounds can be used with many of the lessons from chapters 2, 3 and 4. The best use of the terrain can be gained when a student with physical disability is teamed with an able-bodied one. Street orienteering (p109) can also be fun. Braille compasses are available for the partially sighted or blind although their use is limited to following the cardinal directions, north, south, east and west.

Imaginative planning using a suitable area (and possibly a braille map) could make orienteering a beneficial activity for developing confidence in travelling independently, e.g. star exercise (p36). Aspects of mental fitness (p119), such as the mental rehearsal of routes to be travelled and positive thinking, can contribute to reducing the anxiety experienced by a blind person embarking on an independent trip.

Pupils at the Royal Blind School, Edinburgh have orienteered successfully on a 3 dimensional, tactile map made from a process called 'Thermoforming'. Changes in texture indicate different ground surfaces. Permanent controls marked on the map can be used for selected courses.

String courses (p38,133), picture maps (p25) and simple games have been used successfully with persons who have learning difficulties. Collecting something from each control is more easily achieved than copying down a letter. Matching colours or

pictures is another alternative. When planning lessons for this group objectives should be clear taking into consideration the low levels of literacy, numeracy, the very short concentration span and the need for constant supervision. A 'treasure hunt' with obvious clues solved by following a taped route or chalked arrows can provide a new and enjoyable experience.

Chapter 14 suggests how Trail Orienteering has been developed to meet the need of persons who are not physically able to cross rough orienteering terrain. It also suggests approaches for introducing and developing map skills for persons with learning difficulties.

Parents

Orienteering is an ideal family sport but only if all the family enjoy it. Many of the classroom or playground lessons (and especially the games) can be used to introduce the concepts of understanding plans and maps to young children. They can also be the answer to summer party games or to brightening up a barbecue - make the fit and experienced go three-legged, for example. Many back gardens have been the venue of major 'championships'.

Developing basic skills in the house or garden can give a lot of confidence and support to those first outings in the forest where initial success is vital to continued interest. Always remember that at all stages it must be fun to do. Try some of the following:

INDOORS (p15,16,18,19)	GAMES (Chapter 8)
	Card games (p95)
OUTDOORS	Jigsaws (p94)
Picture maps (p25)	'O' bingo (p98)
Mini map races (p33)	Shake a dice (p99)
Relays (p28)	'O' twister (p100)
Surprise map drawing (p67)	
Team score event (p43)	

PRACTICAL PREPARATIONS

Plan a programme

Plan a course of lessons and arrange transport if necessary (see 'aims and objectives' p5).

Plan exercises and games for the first 3 lessons.

Before starting a programme

MAPS: prepare classroom, playground and/or local area maps (ch 13), or obtain local park/woodland orienteering maps - if they exist (p153).

CONTROLS: Make or buy orienteering control markers. Improvised markers should be painted orange/red and white and made as distinctive as possible e.g. old detergent containers, 1 gallon plastic squash containers or plastic cups. See Classroom Project 1 (p124).

PUNCHES: Make or buy control punches or wax crayons (attach string). For permanent courses, or where there is a danger of punches being stolen, pupils will have to carry a pencil to write the code letters onto the control card. A pencil attached to string pinned on to clothing is safe and accessible.

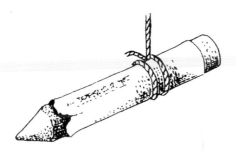

OTHER EQUIPMENT: collect all the other items you need - coloured pencils, adhesive tape, control cards, safety pins, whistles, old orienteering maps from local club (compasses are not needed at first).

VIDEOS/SLIDES: Prepare or collect any visual aids.

Starter packs are available from *Harveys* who also supply the equipment you need for an introductory course.

MAPS FOR MULTIPLE USE

To save time and money maps can be prepared for multiple use. Decide whether to pre-mark a course for regular use or to leave the map clean. Maps covered with transparent adhesive film can be marked up with a spirit-based pen and cleaned with spirit when necessary. Avoid using a ballpoint pen as this dents the surface and the ink is not waterproof.

- Fold or trim the maps small enough to be easily handled.

- Mark the north edge with red and draw a North arrow.

- The legend can be cut off and repositioned if necessary on the trimmed down map.

- Cover with matt self adhesive transparent film, seal in a good quality polythene bag, or laminate.

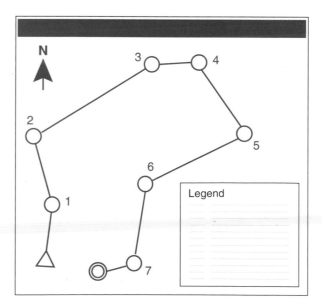

Pre-marked courses:

Descriptions on the front.

Circles drawn with a template (6mm), <u>not</u> freehand.

Write numbers <u>outside</u> circles.

Link circles with lines but do not obscure line features on the obvious routes.

Although giving an extended life, stiff lamination or maps on boards are not recommended because children cannot fold or thumb the map.

HOW TO INTRODUCE ORIENTEERING

The first lesson in orienteering is probably the most important one in catching the imagination and interest of your students. They should experience the feeling of the sport - the excitement of finding control points, successful interpretation of the map and the physical involvement of running between controls.

An attractive visual presentation can contribute a lot to initiating this feeling and wherever possible should be used as part of this lesson.

A straightforward classroom lesson is a useful introduction before progressing outside into playgrounds or woodland: the enclosed space allows close supervision of individual progress and those having difficulty can be helped straight away.

In woodland or forest the 'Direct Method' of teaching (p39) with back-up instruction has proved to be most successful in holding interest. This method does however need a lot of manpower and is impractical for most teachers with a school group.

In planning a programme of orienteering, organisation and preparation are essential especially if you, the teacher or instructor, are on your own. The purpose of this book is to make this job easier

- by giving checklists for skills to be taught as well as for each lesson and exercise,

- by maximising the use of permanent courses,

- by using the school and playground to introduce basic skills, and

- by providing a wealth of ideas for progress with any group.

If you have not already done so, GO ORIENTEERING to experience the sport before you undertake to teach it. You will find it is an exciting individual sport about reading a map and running through the countryside. It is certainly not a group walk with boots on, a treasure hunt or a compass-only exercise. These are all frequent misconceptions.

Courses for the newcomer are planned so that all controls are easily found. The lessons and exercises in this book show you how to plan courses so that your pupils have the satisfaction and enjoyment of finding all the controls.

VISUAL PRESENTATION

What is orienteering? The intention here is to provide beginners with an exciting picture of the nature of the sport.

VIDEO
1 Orienteering - THE FIRST STEPS
   (two 12 minute sections VHS)
   Part 1: Orienteering at school
   Part 2: Out in the forest
2 Challenge to Sport - Orienteering
   (8 minutes VHS)
3 Orienteering skills
   (5 parts total 59 minutes VHS)

Contact your national orienteering federation or Harveys for up-to-date information on videos available (addresses p153).

SLIDES
Harvey Starter Pack, set of 6 slides as on p3.
Your local club may have a set showing aspects of competition.

PHOTOGRAPHIC DISPLAY
Setting up this type of display can be done as part of the lesson then left up for closer observation.

WALL CHART
For further information on visual aids see p153.

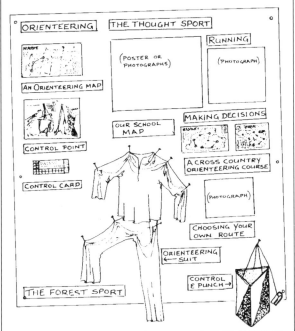

13

2

INTRODUCING ORIENTEERING IN THE CLASSROOM

GETTING STARTED

AIMS
* *to create an interest in orienteering*
* *to introduce the map, map setting, north, control points and circles*

EQUIPMENT CHECKLIST
See page 1 for the key to these symbols

Preparation

Draw a plan of the classroom showing tables, desks, cupboards, etc. Avoid cluttering the map with too much detail. The map should have numbered boxes down the side.

Lesson

Start with a **visual introduction** and a brief description of the sport (p13).

Give out **plans of classroom** - identify the features included on the map - tables, desks, etc.

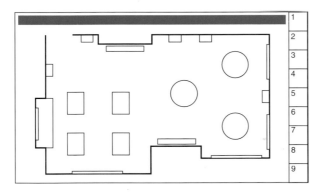

Introduce setting (orientating) the map - keeping the map turned so that map north is always to the north end of the room. By doing this features on the map and in the room are in the same relative position/direction. This makes navigation from one feature to another much simpler.

Mark the north side of classroom map in red. A large N hung on the wall will help orientation.

Put 10 mini-controls (with code letters) on distinctive features in the room, e.g. <u>corner</u> of a desk, <u>side</u> of a window. Be precise, do not hide them. Try to keep all the controls the same height from the ground.

Each pupil marks their own place with a triangle (the orienteering symbol for the start). To mark each control they put a finger by the correct feature on the map, then draw a circle with the number alongside.

clear circle and number on precise point ✓

circle on imprecise point

number obscures point

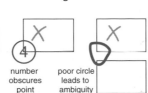

poor circle leads to ambiguity

Practical

Introduce what to do:

"See how quickly you can find each control and mark the letters down the side of the map."

"Sit down when you have finished, 10 points for each control."

"There are 10 controls. Visit them in any order, everyone should get 100 points."

The teacher checks pupils are keeping their maps set by seeing that the red bars on the maps are all to the same side of the room. This makes it easy to spot those who need help.

Further work

Explain the difference between **point to point** and **score orienteering**.

POINT TO POINT

A small number of controls (commonly 6-12) are set out and must be visited in <u>numerical order</u> 1-2-3-etc. The best orienteer is the one who finds all the controls in the shortest time. Missing any controls or going in the wrong order incurs disqualification.

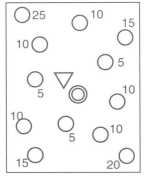

SCORE ORIENTEERING

A fixed time is given to find as many controls as possible <u>in any order</u>. Each control has a points value. A penalty of 6 or 10 points per minute is applied to anyone finishing late. The best orienteer is the one ending up with the highest score.

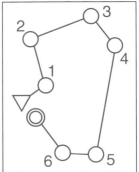

Either of these courses could form the basis of the next lesson and map/control observation exercises.

Progress to a point to point course in the classroom or start orienteering in the gymnasium or playground.

Reinforce map setting.

POINT TO POINT ORIENTEERING

AGE GROUP	7+
TIME	30-45 min

AIMS
- *to introduce point to point orienteering*
- *to establish the concept of map setting*
- *to introduce thumbing the map*

EQUIPMENT CHECKLIST

Preparation

Plan 10-15 control points in the classroom.

Prepare copies of the classroom map and draw the map on the blackboard.

Lesson

Give out one classroom map each. Put out the 10-15 mini controls while pupils mark them on their map in pencil. Do not number them. A master copy is on the blackboard.

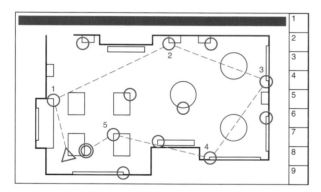

Pupils pair up; each pupil marks a start triangle on the map in their own place, and a double circle (finish) in their partner's place.

The teacher demonstrates a selection of 5 controls to make up a point to point course, numbered 1 to 5. Each pupil then does the same, using the start and finish on their own map.

Pupils swap maps and change places. They then visit the controls in order, writing the code letter down beside each circle. They finish at their own seat.

Remind them always to keep the map set - see previous lesson.

HOLDING, FOLDING, THUMBING THE MAP

By holding a folded map with your thumb beside your chosen route the ability to focus on a reduced area of map is greatly improved. This skill increases the fluency of orienteering as less time is spent stopping and searching for your location on the map. It also decreases the possibility of locating incorrectly and consequently getting lost.

Folding the map to a compact size will help later on when the compass is introduced.

Hold the map in front of you so that the line from the start towards control 1 points away from you. Turn around until the map is set and you are facing control 1. Proceed to the control.

Hold the map so that you are looking through control 1 to control 2. Turn to face control 2 with the map set. Hold the map so that your thumb is beside control 1 - where you are now, if your thumb will not reach, fold the map to help you. Proceed to control 2.

Hold and fold the map so that you are facing control 3, etc.

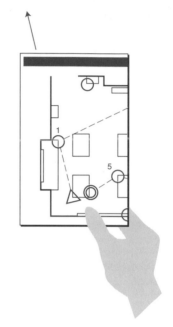

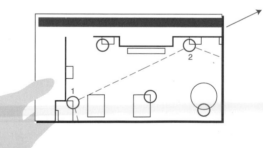

Further work

Progress to Playground Lessons or Star Exercise (p27).

SCORE ORIENTEERING

AGE GROUP	7+
TIME	20-30 min

AIMS
* to reinforce the concept of map setting
* to introduce score orienteering

EQUIPMENT CHECKLIST

Preparation

Prepare a classroom map with numbered control points. Produce enough photocopies for one to each pupil.

Draw the plan on the blackboard or have a stock of enlarged plans to display.

Lesson

Introduce score orienteering (p15).

Give each pupil a number and a mini-marker (or one between two) to stick in the correct position according to their number (see blackboard).

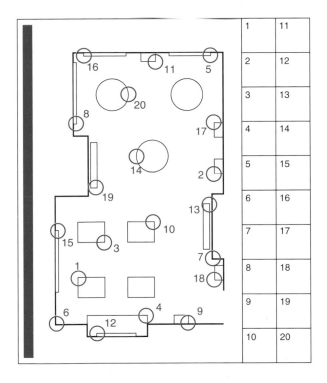

Practical

Pupils have 5 or 10 minutes to find as many controls as possible in any order. 10 points for each control.

The teacher helps those having difficulty, checks answers and counts up scores. Pupils collect controls.

A penalty is not necessary for the classroom exercise.

Adaptations

1 Pupils could plan their route starting first with the number they put out.

2 Divide the class into two teams, each team to get all the controls but the first to finish should help the less able in their team.

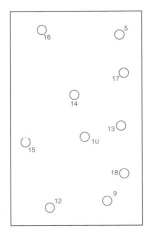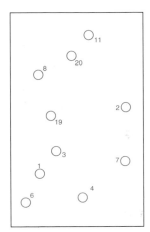

3 Two teams - 2 classroom plans on the blackboard. Each member of team A selects a control point, puts out a mini-marker and marks it on the A master map. Team B does the same. The teacher checks that they select different control sites.

Team A locates all Team B's controls and vice versa.

Use blackboard maps only.

Each team could use different coloured markers. A could use cupboards, doors, chairs, B could use windows, desks, heaters etc.

Further work

The same exercises can be done in the playground.

LINE ORIENTEERING

AGE GROUP   8+
TIME   20-30 min

AIMS
* *to encourage map-ground observation and thumbing the map*
* *to keep the map set whilst changing direction*

EQUIPMENT CHECKLIST

The object of line orienteering is to follow on the ground a line drawn on the map. If the line is followed accurately control markers will be found at various points. Pupils then have to mark the positions of the controls on their maps.

String orienteering (p31,38) is line orienteering with the line marked on both the ground and the map.

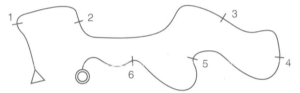

Lines can be set out with or without any controls. With no controls the objective is solely to follow the line. This is the best way to introduce line orienteering in the classroom or playground.

Preparation

Using a classroom map (or just a simple plan of 6-10 objects - gymnastic apparatus, cones, chairs, benches), devise and draw a line for each pupil, plus 3 spare for changeovers. Set out controls (if required) - ensure that every line passes through each control.

Number each map.

Lesson

Each child must follow the line on their map, (finding and marking the position of controls). If necessary walk the group round one course showing them how to thumb the map, follow the line (and find controls).

Stop everyone occasionally, ask them to identify where they are, then continue. Keep swapping maps to give variety. Help those having difficulty.

Adaptations

Gymnasium: put out apparatus of various shapes keeping the layout simple. Pupils draw in the apparatus, showing the shapes.

Everyone chooses a starting position, then creates and draws a line, walking it in the process. When complete change maps and run round different lines.

Playground: pupils copy the line from a master map. Use 3-5 different lines to avoid following.

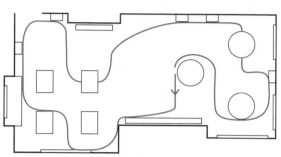

1 Classroom line - pupil designed. No controls. Pupils could start at their own seats.

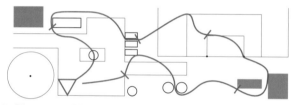

2 Playground line with controls. Pupils follow the line and mark the controls on the map.

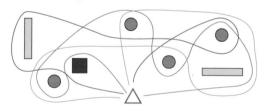

3 Pattern of 7 objects in hall, gym or playground. No controls. Use same start and finish for all lines.

4 Use trees or natural objects outside. 3 and 4 can be used as a team or relay game - short lines and lots of turns.

Further work

Progress from inside to outside, short to longer legs, without, then with controls.

Mini map races. Labyrinth orienteering. Fine orienteering. Line event. String orienteering.

UNDERSTANDING MAPS

AGE GROUP   9+
TIME   30 min +

AIMS
* to develop an understanding of the map as a symbolised picture of the ground
* to make a simple map
* to teach setting the map

EQUIPMENT CHECKLIST

Preparation

Ask the children to bring in a number of personal belongings to use as map features i.e. a comb, pencil case, ruler, ball.

Ensure each child has a sharp pencil and plain white paper.

Lesson

The teacher should lay out an arrangement of objects on a desk ensuring a variety of shapes and sizes. Make the arrangement simple enough for the children correctly to map them.

Ask the children to imagine that they are flies on the ceiling looking down on the desk and to draw in the shape of the desk and then the objects on the desk. Stress the need to get objects pointing the correct way.

Check that they have understood and that their maps are roughly correct.

Teach them to set the maps so that what is to the left on the table is to the left on the map, etc.

Have them approach the desk from different directions and check that their maps are set.

Repeat the exercises letting the children create their own maps using desks pushed together in a group.

Rearrange the objects to create new maps.

Further work

DRAWING A PLAN OF THE CLASSROOM

Draw a plan of the classroom to introduce the concepts of scale.

Discuss symbols and representation of objects on a plan.

A simple way to introduce this is to give each child a sheet of plain paper and ask them to draw an outline of the classroom (just the walls) as a fly would see it looking down from the ceiling.

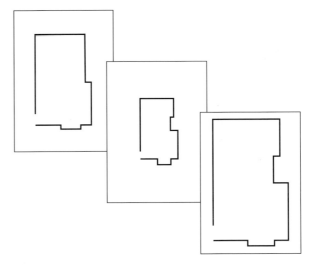

A glance at the results should show a variety of sizes but roughly the same shape.

Explain that the drawings all represent the same room but that the <u>scale</u> is different.

Measure the walls of the room with the class and decide on a scale to fit the paper, e.g. 1:25 (2cm = 1 pace of 50cm).

The outline can then be drawn and the furniture and objects added to each child's plan.

Apparatus in a hall or gymnasium can be plotted in the same way.

For orienteering exercises it is better if everyone uses copies of the same plan.

Discuss maps in general asking the children to bring in a selection ranging from town plans, OS/USGS maps, world maps, architects plans etc.

Build up a collection and display about the classroom.

TABLE TOP PLANS

AGE GROUP	6-8
TIME	30-40 min

AIMS
* *to introduce the concept that maps and plans are a pattern of shapes*
* *to reinforce the concept that a map is like a picture*

EQUIPMENT CHECKLIST
models of houses, trees, fences

Preparation

Collect landscape models or objects with clear and contrasting shapes.

Lesson 1

* Place three objects on a sheet of paper in a very simple pattern. Draw round each piece then remove the objects to show the outline shapes. Discuss which shape matches which object and what shape each one is. A plan has been produced of the model.

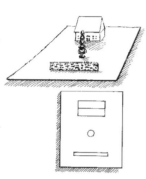

* Place the objects in a different relationship. Draw the correct shapes on a piece of paper next to the model. Involve the children in deciding what shape to draw and where it should go. If the map is to be correct the drawing must match the model.

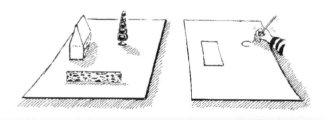

* Give out paper and ask the children to draw the correct shapes lying in the right direction. Place the objects on a central table, or use a number of sets of objects with smaller groups of children.

These games and exercises can be adapted to suit the needs and ability of your particular group of children. For example, the children of a class which understands these ideas quickly could practise walking toward a piece of apparatus from different parts of the area, keeping the plan set as they move.

Lesson 2

Prepare by drawing a simple picture map and a plan of a table top model, or copy the ones shown on p25.

* Set up the model to match the map. Give each child a copy of the picture map. The children should stand or sit round 3 sides of the model so that they can relate their picture maps to the model. Ask them to set their maps and identify each of the houses and trees.

* Introduce the model car, which is going on a tour, visiting each of the houses. As the car is directed along its route the children follow where it goes on their picture maps.

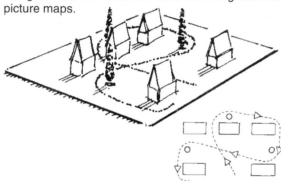

* Choose a new starting point. The children now *draw* in the route the car takes as it goes from house to house. A piece of string showing the route on the model will help them to draw the correct line. Arrows on the line will show the direction the car is going.

* Give each child a plan of the model. Compare and match the picture map and the plan with each other and with the model. Identify the symbols showing trees and houses. Set the plan. Locate the start point of the route shown by the string and already drawn on the picture maps.

* Draw the route on to the plan by looking at the line of the string. Compare it with the line on the picture map.

Adaptations

Put an x underneath an object. Show the class where it is on the plan and ask them to identify which object it is under.

Place coloured paper on corners of objects. The children mark their plan with the correct colours.

Further work

Children can make their own models and then make maps or plans of them. Plot in routes using string, and then transfer them onto the maps.

MASTER MAP COPYING

AGE GROUP   9+
TIME   30-40 min

AIM
* *to teach accurate copying from master maps*

EQUIPMENT CHECKLIST

At major orienteering events competitors are provided with a map with their course pre-printed. At small events a master map of each course is displayed for competitors to copy on to their own map. Competitors copy the course as part of their total race time - the master maps are usually positioned just after the start.

Beginners frequently copy the control circles incorrectly. Teaching them how to transfer the course accurately will save the frustration of looking in the wrong place for a control marker.

Preparation

Obtain lots of orienteering maps, out of date ones will do - ask your local club.

Plan and draw up a number of point to point courses with 5-8 controls (yellow-orange standard) on a variety of line features - use a circle template.

Write out a control description list for each course.

Lesson

Explain the purpose of master maps. Stress the importance of accuracy in copying the course. Use a blackboard or overhead slide to show how to copy.

Put the index finger of one hand on the control on the master map. Put the index finger of the other hand on control site on your own map.

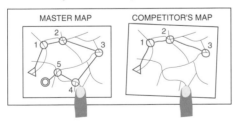

Double check with the control description list that the correct feature has been identified.

Draw a circle carefully - a single line, not several.

Write the control number in same place as on the master map.

Master maps are usually mounted on boards with space to one side for copying.

Practise copying a course with no time limit (one master map can be shared between two pupils if master maps are limited).

Note

Draw circles carefully with a fine pen.

Include start and finish.

Put numbers outside the circles to avoid obscuring detail.

Put a dot by the feature if the circle does not make the location clear.

Link the circles.

Check that all controls are copied and numbered.

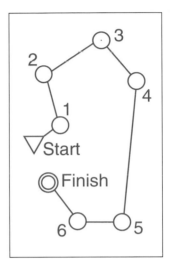

Adaptation

Make a team competition by running the length of a hall and copying one control at a time.

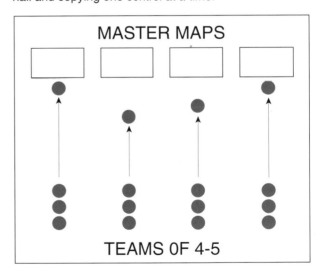

Further work

Theory lessons
Orienteering games
Contour and compass work
Project work

Note: Children under 12 should always have their maps checked once they have copied their course from a master map in a competition.

21

TREASURE ISLAND

AIMS
• to establish the meaning of the word "set" and follow up the use of shapes and symbols

AGE GROUP 6-8
TIME 30-40 min

EQUIPMENT CHECKLIST
clipboards, objects to use as features (lake - water basin, etc.)

Preparation

Collect equipment. Decide the size of area to use: younger children need to be able to overlook the whole area; older ones can use a larger area with bigger features. Read a story about an island.

Lesson

• Give out paper, boards, coloured pencils. Seat the children round the area to be used for the island.

• Using chalk or rope, mark out the coastline of the island in a simple shape. As you add features on the island, the children draw them on their own paper. A mixture of pictures and symbols is quite acceptable for this map.

• Place large features first: a lake (basin of water) and river (blue cord) leading to it; a box as the house; cones (or pot plants) can represent trees; a chair can be a lookout tower. A field (outlined with canes or rope) can be used to fill in the gaps.

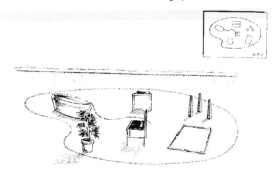

• Story line: following a shipwreck a box of treasure is buried. Before being rescued the mariners make a map of the island so that the treasure can be found later. The children are the shipwrecked mariners.

Ask the children to bury their treasure somewhere on the opposite end of the island. Mark the place with a T.

Now years later you return to dig up your treasure. You land on the island at the point where you are sitting. Mark it on your map with an arrow.

t = treasure

• "Which route will you take to get to the treasure?" The teacher demonstrates. Plan the route looking at the model, then trace it on the map with a finger. The map must be kept set to follow the route.

A few children can talk through the route which they would follow, identifying the features they will pass by pointing at the model or the map.

• If the island is big enough, the children can then try to follow the route, walking from one feature to the next until the treasure is reached.

Adaptations

Use the playground for a large island.

Follow up

Talk about islands. Collect information about islands such as Australia, Britain or Iceland. Make maps of other areas or models.

This is an ideal starting point for cross-curricular work.

3

SCHOOL OR CENTRE GROUNDS

All these exercises and lessons can be taught using picture maps (p142). Many can be done in the classroom (see chapter 2) or used in parks or woodland.

MAP WALK AND SCORE EVENT

AGE GROUP   8+
TIME   30-60 min

AIMS
- *to create an interest in the sport of orienteering*
- *to introduce the concepts of the map and map setting*

EQUIPMENT CHECKLIST

Preparation

Collect school maps (enough for one for each pupil), coloured pencils, paper to write codes on.

Plan ten easy score controls with 10 points each. Pre-mark maps (draw one and copy it). Always use a circle template for drawing controls.

Lesson

Start with a **visual introduction** and a brief description of the sport (p13).

Give each pupil a map and identify all the main features.

Go for a **map walk** - a short walk to relate map to ground and look at some of the control points. The purpose of this could also be to colour a black and white map - colouring makes the map clearer and helps pupils identify areas they colour.

A simple **score** event as individuals or in pairs allows the teacher to help those having difficulty understanding the map. Mini-controls and code letters are the easiest to organise.

Challenge the group to find as many controls as they can but do not make it too competitive e.g. give a time limit but no penalties.

Hang all the controls at the same height above ground level to make them easier to find - do NOT hide them.

Encourage individual participation from the beginning.

With children over 12 years old pairs can be sent to put out the controls, then wait for the teacher to check their position. If this is done the class should gather in one place until all controls are out. Pupils can collect the controls they put out.

Check the codes are correct then discuss achievements and problems.

Explain the difference between score and point to point (normal) orienteering (p15).

Adaptations

An outdoor centre or camp could have a permanent course and pre-marked sealed maps for this lesson (p51)

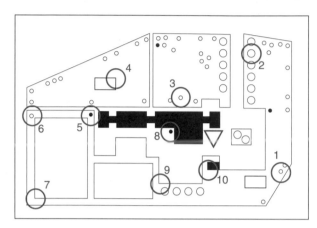

Black and white school map with score controls

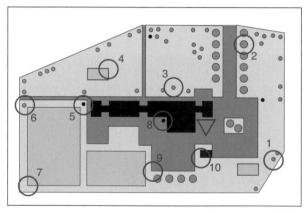

Hand coloured map: brown - roads, orange/yellow - hard areas (tennis courts, etc.) - see map symbols p141.

Further work

A star exercise makes a good follow up or alternative to the score exercise (p27).

A 2-person relay is good fun, introduces point to point orienteering and challenges pupils to find controls in a familiar area (p28).

Follow the tapes (p31) - a good evaluation exercise to see if pupils can identify points on the map.

See score orienteering (parks and woodland) (p37).

PICTURE MAPS

AIMS
• to introduce the sport of orienteering to very young children
• to encourage learning the concept of a map being a picture of the ground

EQUIPMENT CHECKLIST
jigsaws

Preparation

Make or obtain a supply of picture maps of the school.

If the original map is black and white, colour in areas of grass/woodland/concrete for clarity.

Make up 2-4 jigsaws using card or wood. Each piece should have a distinctive feature on it.

Plan 6-8 control sites on distinctive features.

Put out controls and punches.

Lesson

Dry weather is preferable.

Discuss the most distinctive features of the school and grounds
- 'if you were describing the school to a friend of yours ...'

Give groups of 4-6 a mixed up jigsaw. Identify the major features as the jigsaw is put together.

Take the group outside without the maps and look for control markers
- 'what features are they hanging beside?'

Back in the classroom, give out maps. Identify the features where controls were seen, mark with red circles and number them. Draw in a start triangle and the finish circles.

Explain to the group that they have to look at the picture to see in which order to find the controls - 1, 2, 3, etc. Station an older pupil, parent or teacher at the first control - and others if possible. Their role is to ask what features they are looking for, and help punch their cards if necessary.

Set off in pairs, giving time for both children to punch cards before the next pair set off. Timing is not necessary.

If time permits, send them round again (same course). Time them on this occasion.

Adaptations

Use a taped route or string (p31,38). Mark the route on the picture maps. Children have to follow the route and identify the position of the controls.

Further work

Continue using the picture map to find controls. Introduce setting the map if they are not doing so naturally.

Introduce a plan/map of the school, matching map to ground, building on the principle of identifying the feature to find the control.

Work with desktop maps (drawing shapes of objects) and a classroom plan (p19).

SETTING THE MAP

AGE GROUP | 8+
TIME | 20-30 min

AIM
• *to establish the concept and advantages of setting the map*

EQUIPMENT CHECKLIST
ropes, benches

Preparation

A plan of the school field is needed. Extra objects (benches, bins etc.) can be added and drawn accurately onto the plan (see red objects below).

Lesson

Pupils practise setting their map to the ground using both the permanent features (games pitch) and the temporary ones (benches added by teacher).

Once set, features on the map and on the ground are in the same relative position. This makes navigation/direction finding from one feature to another simpler.

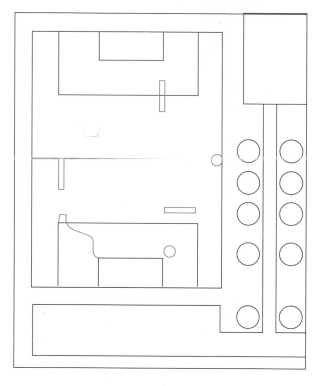

Adaptations

The teacher puts out extra objects and pupils have to draw them accurately onto their plan.

The teacher draws extra objects on the plan and pupils have to put them out in the correct place.

The pupils do the above in two teams - one draws, one puts out.

Further work

To make these exercises more difficult, use a larger scale plan and only show the temporary objects. The pupils must then look at the orientation of the objects in order to set their plan, without the help of a large feature such as the games pitch.

Such a plan can also be used for the adaptations of the exercise.

Try a star exercise or any other exercise in this chapter.

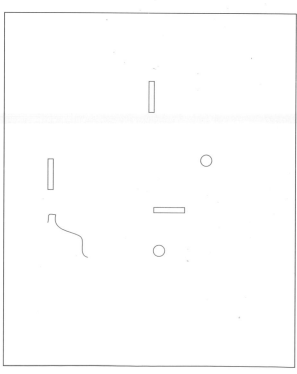

STAR EXERCISE

AIMS
* *to give pupils confidence to navigate alone*
* *to challenge everyone in a mixed ability group*
* *to enable the teacher to identify and help the slower learners*

EQUIPMENT CHECKLIST

Preparation

Draw a master map with all controls (10-15) within 300 metres of a central base - the starting point.

For each control draw 2 'control maps' showing the start, the control, its description and the code letter(s). There should be at least one per pupil. Keep the map small and protect it in polythene or with adhesive covering if it is to be used again.

Prepare a check sheet (see example opposite).

Put out the controls with punches/crayons and code letters.

Make a master control card for checking.

Name	1	2	3	4	5	6	7	8	9	10	
Katy	/	/		/	/	/		/			
Tom			/	/	/		/	/		/	
James	/			/	/	/		/	/		/
. . .											

CHECK SHEET

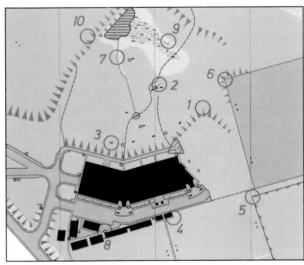

MASTER MAP

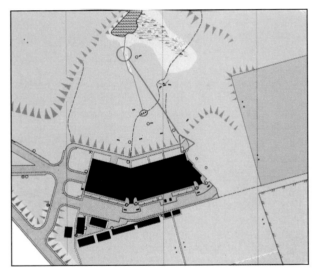

CONTROL MAP

Lesson

Explain how the exercise works:

Pupils work individually. Give each pupil a number, the appropriate control map, and a control card.

Everyone goes to the starting point (triangle on map). On the whistle they go and find their control, punch the card (control 4 in punch box 4), and return to the start.

Instruct any less able or younger ones that they must set the map first and face in the right direction. Check them before they leave the start.

Keep changing maps. Check the master and tick off on a check sheet after each visit (two staff or a non-active pupil could help here).

Finish when appropriate and have pupils fetch controls.

Adaptations

Make up some control maps with 2-4 controls on them. Introduce these to more confident pupils once they have found a couple of single controls.

More experienced pupils could do this exercise as 'map memory' (no map), and more competitively e.g. to get all controls.

This is an ideal exercise for introducing a group to a new area or a new technique.

Further work

Progress to a simple relay or point to point event working individually. Use some or all of the same control sites for very young groups.

Remember: success breeds confidence.

POINT TO POINT ORIENTEERING

AGE GROUP   9+
TIME   30-60 min

AIMS
- *to practise setting the map and relating map to ground*
- *to present the sport of orienteering in a limited environment*

EQUIPMENT CHECKLIST

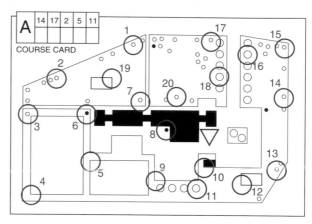

Preparation

Plan 4-5 point to point courses with 5 controls each. If the school field is devoid of features add some temporary objects (cones, benches, etc.) and mark them on the map.

Draw up a master map with start and finish and all 20-25 controls. Use a circle template. Number each circle. Make a copy for each pupil.

Prepare a sheet of course cards showing the different sequence of controls. Make the same number of copies as maps, preferably on light card. Cut out into separate courses. Keep one card complete to serve as an answer sheet.

Hanging crayons or punches make it more like real orienteering, otherwise controls can just have code letters to be copied (perhaps the correct control number plus a code letter). If a code letter has to be copied, each pupil will need a pencil - ideally on a string pinned to the clothing along with the control card.

Practical

Give out a map to each pupil. Share out the control markers between pairs of pupils who then go and hang them in the correct places and return to the start. Demonstrate how to tie or hang the control. Some may have to be tied to a cane and stuck in the grass.

Distribute the course cards (one each). Write names and start times on the back and pin to waist or leg.

The course can be run or walked individually or (younger pupils) in pairs. Controls must be visited in the correct order - the sequence shown on each card. Pupils copy the code letters or punch the card.

Set off 4 or 5 at a time. The teacher times them back and pupils can calculate their own elapsed time. Use any children unable to do the course to help with the timing, or have a large clock and encourage pupils to time themselves.

When one course is finished and checked, a new one is started. Times can be compared for each course although the emphasis should be put on having the right answers.

Adaptations

- The code letters for each course can make up a word or anagram.

- Fewer courses can be set out for smaller groups. The disadvantage of only one short playground course is the waiting - before the start, and early finishers.

- **Map memory**. A master map of each course is at the start - pupils have to remember all 5 controls. Use this with older pupils familiar with the map.

- **Night** orienteering - safe introduction for youngsters.

Further work

The same map can be used for a score event. 20-25 controls, with 10-20 minutes to find as many controls as possible in any order. 10 points for each control, 10 point penalty for each minute late (blow a whistle when there are 2 minutes left). Give each pupil a different control to start with.

Head to head race. *Pair off the group according to ability. One races round a course one way, his partner goes the other way. First back is the winner. This is a good way to end a lesson using controls already visited.*

2 - 3 person relay. *Plan 2 or 3 courses that can be done both ways. Pre-mark the maps. Have a mass start for first leg runners, using the control card as the 'baton'. This needs careful organisation but is good for encouraging team spirit. Each team runs the courses in a different order to avoid following (team 1: ABC, team 2: BAC, etc). Mark team control cards to make the order clear. Give out maps before the start to allow plenty of time for everyone to understand the system. Teams can select their own running order (leg 1 - cool under pressure of a mass start, leg 2 - mainstay of the team, leg 3 - the athlete ready for a sprint finish).*

Relays (p47).

POINT TO POINT COURSE

AIM
• *to introduce older pupils to the most common form of orienteering in a familiar area*

EQUIPMENT CHECKLIST

Preparation and practical

Prepare a master map and list of control descriptions as shown.

Set out the course using markers identified with code letters of a suitable size.

Pupils copy the course and control descriptions down and are set off at 1 or 2 minute intervals. A start list is useful. They are timed back and results calculated.

Any mistakes or controls missing - add a time penalty, say 5 minutes per control, rather than disqualify.

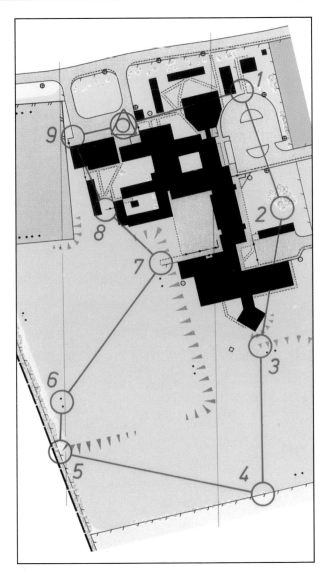

CONTROL DESCRIPTIONS		
1	AB	Fence end
2	AT	Trees, south end
3	BZ	Foot of steep slope
4	CG	Tree
5	CD	Old fence, steep slope
6	AX	Goal post
7	AZ	Path end
8	TL	Wall end
9	BN	Field corner

Adaptations and further work

This type of course (point to point) is the most common type of orienteering and all the other exercises are an adaptation of this basic model aimed at giving more experience and helping students to improve significantly.

Further work might involve using more detailed maps with point to point courses.

Progress by setting different route choice problems in the same area once map orientation and feature recognition have been established.

Introduction to new areas or local club competitions will add considerable interest and experience.

NB *Do not presume that the whole group has taken in everything the first time.*

Progress slowly using similar features for controls many times.

SCORE ORIENTEERING

AIMS
- *to reinforce setting the map and finding controls in a limited time*
- *to challenge a mixed ability group*

EQUIPMENT CHECKLIST

Preparation

Pre-mark maps, one for each pupil. Use 15-20 control sites. Controls should be numbered.

A permanent course may be used if available. Control cards are needed.

Lesson 1

Use pupils in pairs to put controls out. The controls must be checked.

Explain score orienteering (p15).

Set a time limit - 15 minutes. Controls can be visited in any order. 10 points for each control, -5 for each minute late. Have a mass start.

Revise setting the map. Give each person a control number which they must visit first to stop the whole group going to the same first control. Allow pupils time to plan in which order they will visit the controls.

Use the start and finish as a base to return to if help is needed.

Lesson 2

As a follow on from the above lesson but with different groups. Give each group member a map without any controls marked on, and a pencil. Then, individually or in pairs, challenge them to find all the controls which are out and mark them accurately on their map. 10 points for each one correctly marked. Give a time limit. Staff can help those having difficulty.

Further work

Teams can compete - either all controls between the team, or first team to finish with every member to find all controls.

SCORE EVENT
Control descriptions

Time limit 30 minutes
5 point penalty
    for every minute late
Each control punched
    scores 10 points

1   Fence, E. end
2   Corner of trees
3   Path junction
4   Flower bed, E. end
5   Climbing frame
6   Copse, S.E. end
7   Building, N.E. corner
8   Monument
9   Wall, N.W. corner
10 Flower bed, N. end
11 Clearing, E. end
12 Wood edge
13 Fence corner
14 Trees, N. end
15 Fence corner
16 Bank foot
17 Clearing S. corner
18 Hedge, N. end
19 Pond, S. edge
20 Pylon

Aston Villa
Football Club

PLAY
AREA

S/F

FOLLOW THE TAPES

AGE GROUP   8+
TIME   45-60 min

AIMS
* *to increase confidence in following a route alone*
* *to develop observation of the ground and map together*

EQUIPMENT CHECKLIST

Preparation (allow plenty of time)

Plan a line on the map for the taped route to follow.

Make up a master copy with control circles at distinctive points on the map along the taped route.

Either prepare pre-marked maps or prepare a master map for pupils to copy with <u>only the line</u> shown.

Put out tapes and control markers where marked. Clothes pegs are handy for clipping tapes in place. Small green garden canes with tape attached could be used where there is nowhere for fixing (see string courses p133).

Lesson

Explain how the exercise works. The line on the map has to be followed and, if followed accurately, controls will be found. These should be marked in the correct positions on the map.

Marking the controls in the correct place is more important that the time taken.

Pupils copy the line on to their maps (unless pre-marked).

Set them off at 2 minute intervals with a control card, map and pencil. Too short an interval will cause grouping or following.

Time them round the course if desired.

Have something planned for those waiting to start and for the first ones to finish, e.g. writing down features to be followed along a course marked on an orienteering map, or a game such as a word search (p105).

Adaptations

To make this easier, pupils could draw both the lines and the control circles on their map before they start.

Questions can be set at each control.

> What colour is the gate?
> How old is this house?

The answers should be found at the right location.

To make it more difficult give pupils a blank map. They can draw the line on as they go, or when they return, the latter being more difficult.

As an easier alternative, start with a picture map.

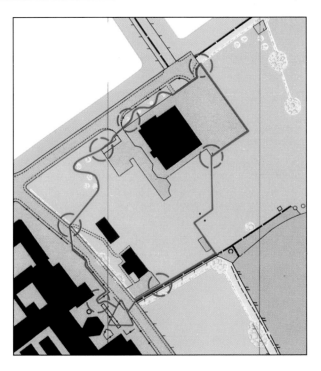

Further work

Similar courses can be set up in more difficult areas such as parks, woods and even large forests.

Controls for beginners should always be placed on large features.

Such work is very successful with younger children as they have fewer worries about being lost with a tape to follow.

String courses for 3-10 year olds are often set up at orienteering events (p38).

Line orienteering (p18) can be usefully adapted to the school grounds, i.e. follow the line on the map without any tapes on the ground.

MAPPING EXERCISE

AIMS
- *to encourage pupils to look at the ground and to relate ground features to their map*
- *to practise estimating 'relative' position*

EQUIPMENT CHECKLIST
clipboards

Preparation

A base map should be prepared showing the main boundaries and features of the area.

For this it is easiest to use a building plan or a topographic map, or to simplify an existing orienteering map.

A key should be prepared showing pupils the recommended symbols and colours.

Everyone will need a clipboard and coloured pencils

Practical

Walk around the area.

Colour areas according to the key - grass etc.

Mark the correct symbols for walls, fences etc.

Plot new features - trees, bushes, seats etc.

Try to make the position and shape of the feature drawn on the map match its position and shape on the ground.

Show steep slopes and/or contours if appropriate.

EXISTING BUILDING PLAN/MAP

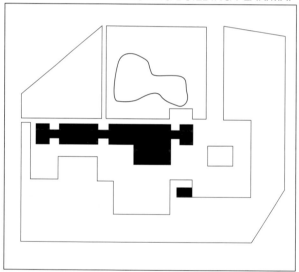

COLOURED VERSION WITH NEW DETAIL

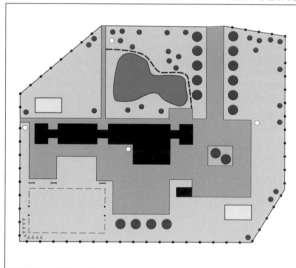

KEY

▨	road	▨	hard area
▨	paved path	▨	grass
- - - -	other path	▬	woodland
🝙	pond	▨	sandpit
•—•—•	wall	• • •	bushes
—•—•—	fence	●	single tree
———	fence	◡	(contour)
–	seat	▾▾▾▾	steep bank
■	building	• •	games posts
○	litter bin	⌐ ¬	playing pitch lines

Adaptations

The exercise can be made easier by just colouring in buildings, grass etc.

It can be made harder by choosing a more complicated area.

To cut down on time the map can be divided into sections and each pupil or pair checks a section. The information can then be drawn onto a master.

Further work

Use the maps drawn by pupils to plan courses. Pupils could swap maps to see if they can interpret other maps.

MINI MAP RACES

AIMS
* *to improve map reading on the move*
* *to increase fitness*

EQUIPMENT CHECKLIST

Preparation

Draw a large scale map of, say, a group of trees, bushes, posts, boulders. Make copies for the group.

Lesson

Ask each person in the group to draw a line on the map weaving round the trees and posts. Number each map.

Work in pairs, alternately following each line. Keep changing the maps. See how many lines can be followed in 10 minutes.

LINE COURSE

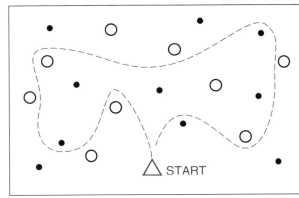

Attach a punch to each feature. Set a series of mini courses - to be done in pairs again.

Control cards are needed.

Use map memory for more experienced students.

MINI COURSE - every post and tree has a punch

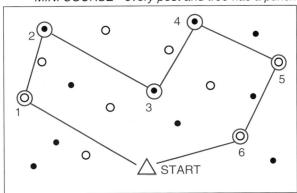

Teams of 3 - 5. Each team starts with a different type of course - punches only, line, map memory, etc. Time how long each team takes and write it down. Move on to the next map and try to beat the best time set by the previous team.

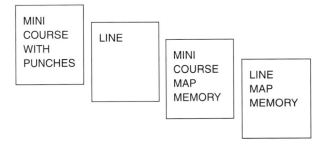

The exercises can be set with cones or other temporary objects, as in line orienteering (p18).

Adaptations

LABYRINTH ORIENTEERING

Set out a maze using tapes or flags or ropes.

Draw a plan and photocopy it.

Set the pupils off through the maze. Encourage them to reset the plan as they turn each corner - and realise that the plan stays facing the same direction - it is the individual who turns around it!

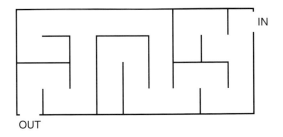

This can also be used to introduce setting the map with a compass - add magnetic north lines to the plan.

Note: do not allow pupils to look at plan for very long before they start otherwise they will work out their route and not need to look at the plan.

Further work

Apply the same skills with orienteering maps.

4

PARKS & WOODLAND

Initially some of the exercises performed in the school grounds can be used in a park or woodland setting e.g. simple star course or point to point orienteering courses. If the school is limited in the availability of such areas these exercises can be planned on the school grounds map to provide some variety.

Many of these lessons and exercises can be used both in the school grounds and in larger woodland areas.

Check access arrangements for the area to be used. It is important to obtain permission from landowners.

Examine again progressions in the step system (p7). The principles of map orientation, recognition of features from the map and route choice decisions take time and experience to establish. After an introductory lesson further work should be planned carefully to ....

  a) introduce new features,
  b) increase experience of specific problems.

example 1: line feature development
- following roads, tracks, paths, observing open woodland changes and buildings.
- including walls and fences.
- including streams, large marshes, clearings.

example 2: problem development
- (no route choice) straight on, left or right, controls at each change of direction.
- (no route choice) obvious line features to follow, controls at change of feature.
- (no route choice) controls further apart, two features to follow.

MAP WALK/TAPED LINE

AIMS
* *to introduce the sport of orienteering*
* *to identify colours and line features on an orienteering map*
* *to establish the principle of setting the map*

EQUIPMENT CHECKLIST

Preparation

Obtain a supply of orienteering maps of a local park or woodland area. The local club will be the best source. Check access arrangements. It is essential to obtain permission from landowners.

Purchase or make a supply of control markers, punching devices (punches/wax crayons) and code letters.

Plan a route for the first lesson - see planning note below.

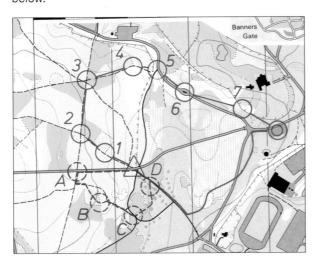

Banners
Gate

```
——— Map walk (controls1-7)
– – – – Taped route (controls A-B-C-D,
         on teacher's map only)
○◁      Control circle (drawn with a template)
         Start
◎       Finish
```

Tapes - strips of polythene, cotton or nylon, tied or pegged

Map walk idea: hang a few cards along the way with questions to keep pupils thinking.

Where are you? Is your map set? Can you see the ditch?	Is your map set? Which way will you follow the ditch?

Planning note: make the walk longer with younger children to give more confidence in map reading. All controls should be white standard i.e. impossible to miss. Use features that are close together with one obvious route. Keep the course short, max. 2.5km.

Pre-mark a map for each child. Cut or fold them so that the unit is as small as possible but still has the legend and scale evident. The children should be able to thumb the map wherever they are.

For long term preservation, cover with clear adhesive film or seal tightly in a polythene bag. Do not put maps on boards. This makes them harder to thumb and fold unless it is a very small piece of map.

Lesson

Start with a brief introduction to the sport.

Hand out maps and (safety) pin control cards on to left wrist (cuff) and explain what is to happen.

On a map walk, teacher and children should identify features on the map and on the ground. Concentrate on the basic colours and line features. Discuss setting the map, observation and thinking.

Following a taped line, children follow a taped route individually or in pairs and identify the location of each control found. They show the teacher the position of controls on their return or mark their maps as they proceed. This can be done as a circuit or by linking directly with the remaining controls.

Finding controls, children do a simple orienteering course, punching and running. Tell them to wait at the finish.

If there is time, walk round and collect controls asking questions that relate the map to the ground.

Note: if the maps are sealed, use a permanent felt tipped pen for marking. This can be removed by wiping with methylated spirit. Ball points indent the surface and are not permanent.

Adaptations

Plan controls in a circuit if you are on your own and do not want them to finish without an adult to supervise. In urban parks younger children should go in pairs.

Further work

A star exercise followed by a short point to point or score competition would be a suitable follow up.

Feature identification games (p95,98,99,106).

MAP WALK/STAR EXERCISE

AGE GROUP	10+
TIME	60 min+

AIMS
- *to introduce the sport of orienteering*
- *to teach recognition of line features and setting the map*
- *to allow individuals to progress at their own pace*

EQUIPMENT CHECKLIST

Preparation

Obtain a supply of maps of a local park or area of woodland. Check access arrangements.

Purchase or make control markers, marking devices (punches or wax crayons) and code letters.

Plan a star exercise and a point to point course:

Star exercise: 8-15 controls within 300 metres of a distinctive central base; plan single and double control maps (see examples).

Point to point course: very simple (white standard) which uses familiar terrain and some of the star controls.

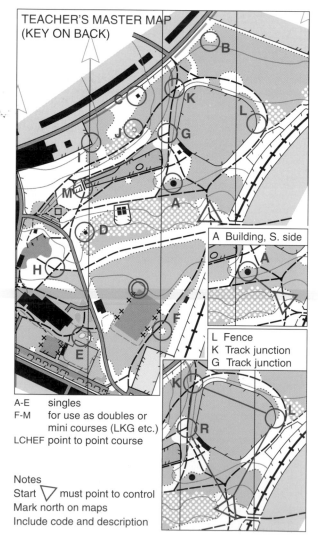

TEACHER'S MASTER MAP
(KEY ON BACK)

A Building, S. side

L Fence
K Track junction
G Track junction

A-E   singles
F-M   for use as doubles or
         mini courses (LKG etc.)
LCHEF point to point course

Notes
Start ▽ must point to control
Mark north on maps
Include code and description

Draw enough single control maps for each pupil to start with one. Draw up doubles and mini courses - the total number should be at least the number in the group. Make more of the easy ones, two of each if working in pairs. Small map sections could be mounted on card.

Set and draw a point to point course and the map walk line on the same map. Include control descriptions.

Prepare a check sheet and identify control maps clearly (A, M, AHB, etc.) for the star exercise.

Put out the controls with punches/crayons and codes. Having two staff members makes the organisation less hectic. If someone else is to put the controls out, tape and label the control sites exactly where you want the control to be hung.

Lesson

Start with a brief introduction to the sport.

Hand out map walk maps and explain the procedure. Take the children on a map walk and familiarise them with map colours, line features and map setting. Show a control marker hanging in the terrain.

Star exercise: take in the maps used for the walk and give out single control maps. Assume individual participation. Check their maps are set before leaving the start. The pupils have to find the right control, punch the card and return to the start. The punch is checked and they swap maps. They should do 2 - 3 single controls each, then progress to mini-courses, again 2 - 3 each. Some pupils could bring controls in.

As they finish the mini-courses, give out a point to point course map, a new control card and set them off. Time them if possible. Ensure that they all wait at the finish.

Discuss and test what was learnt.

Adaptations

This lesson can be adapted well for use at a permanent course.

Further work

A score event in the same area using some of the same controls.

Theory: point to point and score events (p15), route choice (p86), holding and thumbing (p16).

SCORE ORIENTEERING

AIMS
- *to introduce the sport of orienteering to older children and adults in an 'easy' area where there is a shortage of time*
- *to challenge a mixed ability group*

EQUIPMENT CHECKLIST

canes

Score events should have lots of controls (each of which has a different points value according to difficulty/distance) to be found in any order within a given time, e.g. 45 minutes. A penalty is applied for exceeding the time, e.g. -10 pts for each minute late. For introductory score events where finding controls is the main objective, 10 points for every control makes it easier for pupils to decide in which order to visit controls. Beginners will have little concept of how far they can go in a limited time.

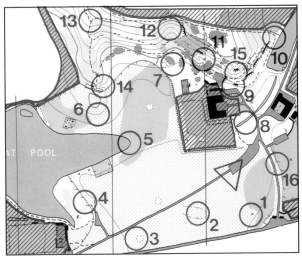

Advantages of score events
- a mass start and limited time make them easy to organise.
- if a control cannot be found or is missed it does not matter.
- ideal introduction in a small area with clear boundaries.
- good for permanent courses.

Disadvantages
- some children may just have no idea where to start, especially if they cannot set the map or recognise features.
- with free choice of controls it is difficult to plan clear routes.
- in an unfamiliar area, beginners can easily get lost and then it can be difficult to locate them. It is easier to keep track of a group on a point to point course.
- this is not the most common form of the sport.

Preparation

Obtain a supply of maps and check access arrangements.

Plan a variety of easy control sites. 10-20 should be enough in a small area (remember you have to put them out - have you got that many?).

Prepare a description list and control card. These can be drawn at the side of a photocopied map.

Put out controls with codes and punches. Use garden canes where there are no trees to hang the controls from. Controls should be clearly visible from all sides.

Premark maps for first lessons. Number controls at random to discourage children from finding them in number order.

Lesson

Start with a brief introduction to the sport. Explain score orienteering.

Give out maps, control cards, descriptions (+ scores). Look at maps, discuss any questions. Stress the importance of keeping the map set.

Walk to the start and finish point via one or two controls - this gives support to those lacking in confidence.

Check watches, calculate the time of return, remind them they can come and ask for help or advice, and start. If it looks as though the whole group would go for the same first control, give each person a specific number to visit first.

Walking about helping pupils is more valuable than just waiting for them to return to the finish, but be prepared for some to find all the controls within the time limit.

Add up scores, check punch patterns and keep a note of those who may not have found very many controls - they will need help in the next lesson. Some children can collect control markers.

Adaptations

Each pupil could be given a set order to visit all or some controls.

Letters could be used instead of punches. Use letters which make a message, perhaps the name of a pop singer or similar idea.

Further work

Map walk, star exercise, point to point course (p36), yellow standard point to point course, e.g. permanent course (p132), team score event (p43).

Map feature identification games or worksheets chapter (chapter 8).

STRING ORIENTEERING

AGE GROUP **4-8**
TIME **30-90 min**

AIMS
- *to introduce the sport to a range of primary age children without leaving behind the very young or less able*
- *to simplify orienteering in a complex area*

EQUIPMENT CHECKLIST
tapes, string 'machine'

Preparation

Obtain a supply of maps and check access arrangements. Picture maps (p142) can be used for string orienteering.

A small section of a map can be redrawn at a much larger scale and copied.

Borrow a string machine from the local club or cut up lots of strips of bright orange material or polythene.

Tie or peg coloured tapes to points along the line.

Keep all the tapes at the same height (children's eye level).

Go to the area and plan the course through the nicest (most runnable) parts of the wood. Link up distinctive and unique features which will make good control points. Obvious changes of direction will also help children locate on the map. 500-1500 metres is a good range of distance.

Allow 30 minutes per kilometre to put out and collect the string.

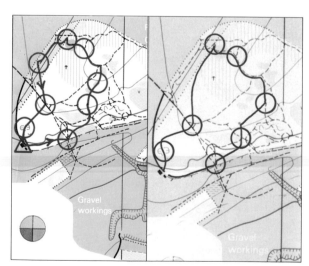

Teacher's map showing control sites.
The black and white copy is slightly enlarged.

Make sure the string will not be a hazard to competitors using the area

Examples of string courses: the aim here is to follow the string which is shown as a line on the map; each control site should be identified and marked on the map ——|—— . Children carry a pencil, or coloured wax crayons can be hung at controls for them to use.

Children under 8 will need a lot of help marking their maps unless it is a picture map. They could be given a map with control circles and encouraged to find the right circle as they come to each control.

Pre-mark the maps with a line. Black and white copies save the expense of using up lots of coloured maps.

Write out and copy control descriptions and stick on the side of the map, or write them on the first map before copying it. Use lower case script.

Put out string or tapes and controls with punches or crayons.

In this exercise the control points are marked on the map. The string or tapes link the controls.

Lesson (dry weather essential)

Start with a brief introduction to the sport of orienteering: "it's a forest, running sport".

Explain the exercise.

Send the pupils round the line with a control card - just follow tapes, run and punch the card. This gives them the feel for finding controls and running through the trees, and also gets rid of surplus energy.

Individually or in pairs follow the tapes with a map each. At each control pupils look where they are and match it with a description, try to find the place on the map - **on the red line**. Mark the spot with pencil or crayon.

(Walk round with the group and check the answers.)

This is particularly suitable for very young children attending events with parents. They often do the same course over and over again.

Adaptations

String courses can be adapted for any age group or experience, e.g. introducing contour features; testing map/ground observation.

Further work

More string or white standard courses until the concept of the map is understood. Combine with playground lessons to increase confidence.

Planning string courses (p133).

DIRECT METHOD

AIM
- *to introduce orienteering directly through the competition*
  First lesson - the feel of the sport, checking codes, punching card,
  finding controls; recognition of tracks and paths, open and woodland

EQUIPMENT CHECKLIST
start, finish banners, results string, safety pins

Preparation

It is essential for this lesson that the teacher has experience of orienteering.

Successful control finding is the main aim without any introductory map walk, so extra manpower or a series of arrows or cards is necessary to stop any wrong turns being taken at critical points.

People helping should be instructed to give minimum advice yet at the same time to encourage independent thinking,

> *"Hold your map so that the track on your map is in line with the track here".*
> *"Which way is the next control?"*
> *"Are you following a path or track to no.4?"*

These questions could also be written on cards. Road beacons or "Go back, wrong way" cards could be placed after critical junctions.

Plan the first lesson's course or courses. Make sure that the controls are close together, especially at any turning points (white standard).

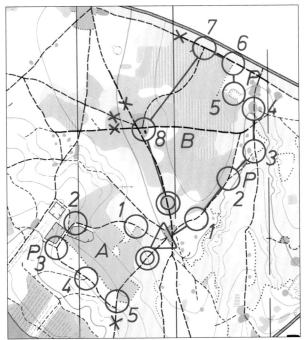

P: person, card or tapes. X: 'Go back, wrong way'

In this area children could complete round A in pairs, then round B on their own if they are feeling confident.

Organisation should take account of the fact that each course will only take 8-15 minutes to complete.

Prepare maps (pre-marked), descriptions and control cards.

Prepare a competition like a real event with a pre-start, start and finish banners, results string (p135). Brief extra helpers.

Lesson (dry weather essential)

- Give a very brief description of orienteering, look at maps - line features and colours. This could be done in a separate session.

- Give out maps, then give out control cards. Write in code letters (from control description list) into each box on the control card, and safety pin to cuff at wrist to keep secure and out of the way. The control descriptions can be with the map or secured with a safety pin to cuff.

- Give each pair a start time. A kitchen clock is useful for display. Use 30 second or 1 minute intervals.

- Encourage running in to the finish. Pupils can then calculate their own time and put stub or card up on a results string.

- Debrief: start to make the children think - do we need practice in map setting, or identification of tracks, paths, green, white, yellow?

- Organise the group to compete on the second course. Alternatively walk round the first course, collect controls and discuss the map, routes, etc.

Further work

Progress with the same system introducing new features to follow on each course, e.g. course C - use ditches and buildings, course D - fences and vegetation. Do not introduce any route choice with the under 12's until you are confident that the majority can set the map by the ground and understand that they must <u>read the map</u> to decide which features to follow.

Debrief/revision periods are an important part of learning. Children should know the aim of each lesson.

If a new area is to be used, go back a few stages to ensure that children do not lose confidence, or allow them to go round in pairs.

Once a small area is exhausted use it for a score event.

Use games to maintain interest in learning (chapter 8).

LINE EVENT

AIMS
- *to encourage pupils to keep the map set all the time*
- *to encourage continuous and detailed map reading*

EQUIPMENT CHECKLIST

In line events the group should be encouraged to concentrate on following a line and reading the map confidently.

Preparation

Prepare two master maps. One is for the students to copy and shows only the line to be followed. The other is for the course planner showing the line <u>and</u> controls.

Following a line demands continuous concentration and tends to be slow. Do not make a line too long, 1-2km is sufficient.

The pupils do not know where the controls are so there is no need for control descriptions.

Set out the course.

Note: a coloured highlighting pen is recommended for drawing lines which follow line features on the map.

Map showing two line loops. Two pupils can start at once, one on each line.

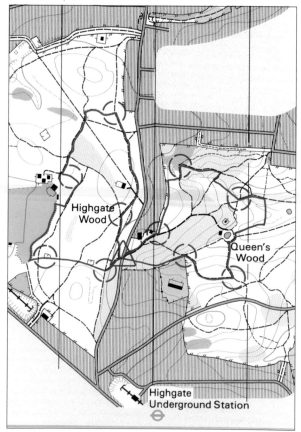

Lesson

Pupils start at 1-2 minute intervals and must follow the line accurately. They punch controls they find on the line and mark their location on the map.

Penalty points can be added for any controls missing or misplaced.

Timing these exercises detracts from careful map reading and should be avoided.

Adaptations and further work

To make this easier for less able pupils tapes can be put out on the line (like a string course).

The course can be made more difficult by changing the route of the line. For example, the line can start off very easy following just roads and paths. As the course progresses the line goes into woods and past smaller features.

ROUTE CHOICE

AIMS
• to teach and encourage route choice decisions - "Which way shall I go?" What do I follow?"
• to demonstrate that the best route between two points is not always a straight line

EQUIPMENT CHECKLIST

Route choice: when many youngsters are introduced to orienteering they do not automatically or naturally appreciate that the answers to the questions *"what do I follow?"* and *"which way shall I go?"* can be found on the map. So initially they should only be looking for one or two line features to follow without *any* route choice.

This exercise can then be used at an early stage to reinforce simple decision making elements - *"shall I follow this path or that wall?"*

With most groups it would be beneficial to look at the course and make the choices indoors first.

Lesson

Students complete the course in pairs - each taking a different route between controls and waiting for each other at the control.

This is just an exercise and should not be timed. However it is possible and interesting to time each leg between controls to note the difference in route choice time. For this extra manpower is needed.

Preparation

Prepare a master map with two or three route options between controls. With younger pupils keep the choice to paths and tracks.

Prepare a control description sheet. Code letters are not entirely necessary but it is wise to use them to familiarise pupils with normal orienteering practice.

Adaptations

This could be set as a star exercise in a suitable area.

Further work

To progress from this exercise more complex route choice problems can be set for the students to figure out for themselves as part of a point to point orienteering course (see below).

Look at a map with 3-4 legs of 'orange' standard showing a variety of route choice using line features (p132).

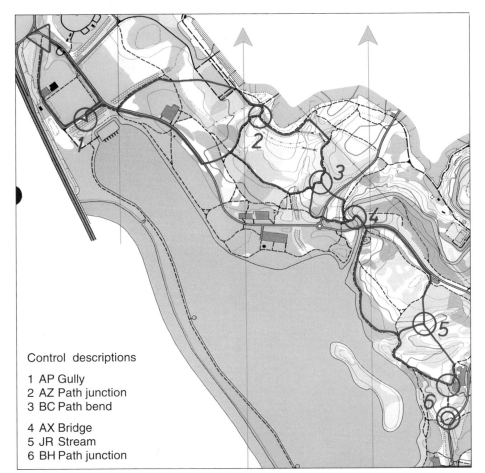

Control descriptions

1 AP Gully
2 AZ Path junction
3 BC Path bend

4 AX Bridge
5 JR Stream
6 BH Path junction

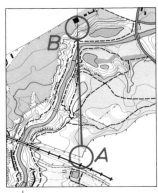

Uncrossable river

ATTACK POINTS - STAR EXERCISE

AIMS
- *to provide practical experience of using an attack point for a hard control*
- *to develop technical expertise in children who have reached orange standard*

EQUIPMENT CHECKLIST

Refer to ATTACK POINTS (p87) for further information.

Preparation

Similar preparation to the star exercise on p36.

Prepare a master map as shown. Red controls are easy and are used as attack points for the harder blue controls.

Prepare maps for each pair of controls (red + blue). Have some spares, e.g. for a group of 15, set 10 legs, make 20 maps - 2 of each.

When planning, take into account the fitness of the group as the return to base is mainly wasted time. For maximum attack point practice keep controls within 300m of the base and attack points within 50m of the control.

Put out controls with codes and punches.

Make a checklist to keep track of everyone.

Practical

Briefly explain why attack points are used.

Gather the group at the central start and give everyone a map. Both controls on any map are to be visited using the red as an attack point for the blue control. They must punch their cards and return to the start. Change maps and repeat.

It might be necessary to revise compass bearings as an accurate bearing should be taken, or how to use the thumb compass for fine orienteering. In both cases it is best to stop and walk in to the control from the attack point, estimating distance and reading every single feature off the map. Pupils should practise having a detailed mental picture of the ground and knowing what feature will catch them behind the control if they miss.

Set a time limit for the exercise.

Adaptations

No compass allowed at all in order to put emphasis on map reading.

Use of the compass from the red to the blue control.

Rather than a control marker put tape out to mark the attack point.

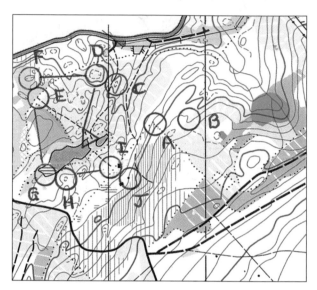

Combine 2-4 legs into a point to point course to finish (see example).

Practise taking a compass bearing from the attack point before reaching it.

Try the exercise using map memory.

Use it as an interval session with very fit groups.

Use for introducing small contour features.

The teacher could write on the back of each map an optimum route choice which pupils can look at if in difficulty or when they get back to the start.

Further work

Plan a point to point course with several alternative attack points and point feature controls.

Omit the attack point circles to allow better pupils to select their own attack points.

TEAM SCORE EVENT

AIM
• to encourage pupils to work together in teams

EQUIPMENT CHECKLIST

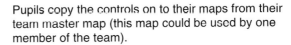

Refer to score event (p37) for further information.

In a team score event all controls have to be collected by teams working as individuals or in pairs. It is an ideal activity for mixed ability teams to encourage pupils to go out on their own.

Pupils copy the controls on to their maps from their team master map (this map could be used by one member of the team).

There is a time limit, e.g. 45 or 60 minutes, and any teams back late receive penalty points, e.g. 10 per minute. The team with the most points wins.

Preparation

Plan a series of 20-25 controls around a central starting point. They should not be arranged in an obvious sequence. Give easy controls low points, more difficult or distant controls higher points.

Adaptations

This idea is good for 'treasure hunt' style orienteering. Use fewer controls but hang a word or letter at each. When pupils return the words give them the final clue

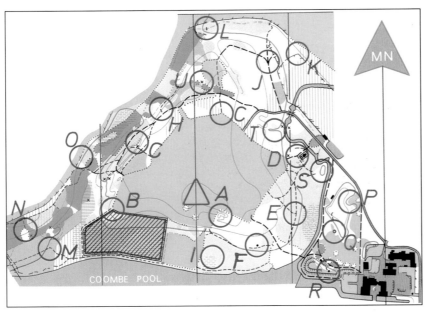

A	Hill top	10
B	Fence corner	10
C	Path end	10
D	Track junction	15
E	Path junction	15
F	Boulder	20
G	Bank foot	20
H	Path bend	20
I	Marsh, N. side	25
J	Track junction	25
K	Fence corner	25
L	Bridge	30
M	Path bend	20
N	Path end	25
O	Fence end	30
P	Re-entrant	30
Q	Monument	20
R	Boulder	25
S	Hill top	30
T	Re-entrant	25
U	Post	30

One master map should be made for each team showing the start/finish and all controls.

Prepare a control description list. The control description list can incorporate the control card.

Set out the markers with appropriate code letters and punch a master card.

as to the position of the 'treasure', or a password (they must find them all - no time limit).

The copying and control collecting decisions can be included within the time limit.

This can be enjoyed in a hall or in the playground.

Lesson

Divide the pupils into teams of 3 or 4, or more.

Give each pupil a map and control card/description sheet.

Each team decides who is going for which controls. A leader could be nominated.

Further work

This can be made more difficult by planning harder controls.

With very able groups a contour-only map could be used for added challenge (p69).

DISTANCE ESTIMATION

AIM
• to link the concept of scale with distance on the ground

AGE GROUP 10+
TIME 60-90 min

EQUIPMENT CHECKLIST
card

Preparation and practical

Prepare two exercises:

1 Indoors. Prepare a map for each pupil with a simple yellow standard course using line features. Alternatively draw a blank course with legs of varying length.

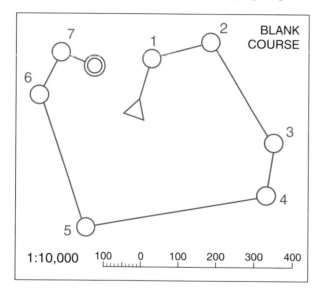

BLANK COURSE

1:10,000 100 0 100 200 300 400

Distance	Estimated	Measured
Start - 1	130	140
1 - 2	150	160

Make up an answer sheet.

Pupils must estimate distance by eye then measure.

Further work

Pacing exercises - see next lesson.

Indoor games (p103).

Indoor work on scale (p84).

Combine with skills learned in point to point courses or the attack point exercise.

2 Outside. Plan and set up a course of 6 - 10 points which can be seen from each other. The legs should be of varying length under 150 metres.

Prepare direction/answer cards as below.

Make up an answer sheet and copy for each pupil. The object is to estimate the distance to each control first by eye then by walking. The answer is found at each control.

Include pacing if the group has already calculated their pace for 100 metres.

↑ Direction to the next control

1 - 2: 320° A compass bearing could be given

2 80m Put the answer on the back of the card at each control

PUPILS ANSWER SHEET NAME:			
Walking pace per 100m = 1 pace =			
ESTIMATED DISTANCE	By eye	Pacing	Answer
S - 1 1 - 2			

PACE COUNTING

AGE GROUP	10+
TIME	30-60 min

AIM
• *to introduce pacing as an accurate means of measuring distance on the ground*

EQUIPMENT CHECKLIST
tape, card

For an orienteer counting double paces, i.e. every right (left) foot, is the most accurate way of checking off distance covered over the ground.

A metre walking pace is most useful for finding controls away from line features, e.g. from an attack point or when the map fails to convey a good picture off the ground.

A running pace is useful, e.g. for finding one of multiple line features, and gives confidence in running through blocks of forest.

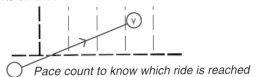

Pace count to know which ride is reached

Pace count to avoid stopping at the wrong ditch

Pace counting is a useful skill for juniors progressing to more technical courses, e.g. green standard, particularly when combined with compass bearings.

Calculate pacing for 10m as well as 100 metres, e.g. 100m - 60 double paces (10m - 6dps).

Divide distances into 100 metre (10m) blocks, i.e. to travel 360 metres,
    running at 60 dps/100m,
    pace 3 x 60 (100m), then 6 x 6 (10m) blocks.

Pacing in blocks of 60 (100 metres) allows for easy adjustment on different types of terrain. Add a few more if you are going uphill or over rough terrain.

Aim for the same walking pace in <u>all</u> terrain.

Teaching points
• Keep paces even
• Don't run too fast
• Don't pace next to someone else
  - you will lose your own rhythm.

PACING NOTES
EXAMPLE

PACING NOTES		
Name: *Jean*		
		100m
300m tape (walk)	180	60
300m tape (run)	144	48
Walking	100m = 60	(10m = 6)
Running	100m = 48	(10m = 5)

Preparation

Plan a lesson using some of the exercises below.

• Measure and mark 100 metres along a path or track. Measure from the map or use a tape. Count paces walking and running and record number taken.

• Put out 200-400m of tapes or string. Pace the whole circuit, then divide into 100m. This gives a better average pace.

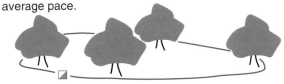

• Star pacing (use as a second or reminder lesson). Put out controls 100m from the starting point, over different kinds of terrain. Make controls visible or use tape along the route.

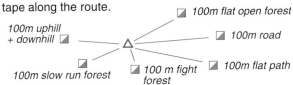

• Star game (pacing and compass bearing). Number the group. Each pupil puts their number, a bearing and a distance on 2 pieces of paper. Leave one piece of

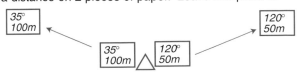

paper at the base. Place the other at the correct bearing and distance on the ground. Keep changing over to find the sheets with the right number.

Further work

Compass and pacing exercises (p82).

Attack points (p42,87).

Traffic lights (p58).

RELOCATION FOR NOVICES

AGE GROUP	8+
TIME	45-90 min

AIM
* *to give beginners confidence to relocate when they get lost thus preventing giving up*

EQUIPMENT CHECKLIST

Basic relocation procedures

8-10 year olds

Lost? Stay where you are. Stay with your partner. Go back to the last control. Do not keep wandering on. Stay on the tracks and paths. Blow your whistle if you are really worried (6 blasts with a pause) and wait until someone comes. This could be at least 30 minutes, so do not worry if no one appears straightaway.

10-16 year olds

Lost? Stop at a distinctive road junction or where two or more features meet. Look carefully at your map and work out which features you followed from the last control. Do any match up with where you are? Could you have gone 180° in the wrong direction? Set the map with the compass and see if you can match the pattern of ground and map.

If this does not work, consider which direction to take to locate yourself on something really distinctive, e.g. north to forest road, west to boundary fence, then south to the road . . .

Preparation

Use an area which is not very familiar to pupils.

Plan a walk along line features passing as many 'unique' junctions as possible.

Have a supply of unmarked maps for each member of the group.

Lesson

Explain the exercise. They are not allowed to look at the map as they walk along but they should look around as they walk and remember as much of their route as possible.

Give out maps and locate the point where the walk starts. Familiarise them with the basic map legend.

Collect the maps in, or ask everyone to fold them up and not to look at them.

Lead the group along a pre-planned route stopping at a distinctive point, e.g. a line feature junction, then ask

* Locate your last known position on the map.
* Set the map with the compass.
* Look around. What features can you see? What features have you followed? Match the pattern of features on the ground to detail on the map.

Start with really easy location points and only make it more difficult if everyone is succeeding in locating themselves.

With pupils aged 12 or over, 'lead them astray into the wood', then tell them to find their way back to the start. They must tell you what they will do before they go. Encourage them to do it on their own. Discuss relocation procedure.

Adaptations

Selected pupils could lead a group to the next location point.

Further work

Plan an easy course. Children work in pairs, with one map. The leader (alternating) stops somewhere between control points; the other takes the map, locates, then navigates to the control and then on towards the next control; stops en route and hands over the map. And so on.

Put out 3-4 controls and punches. Have an unmarked map for each person. Lead the group 'astray' then,

* *ask the children to relocate and meet at control 1. Controls should be marked on maps and given out. The children may need to go out to a large feature to relocate then navigate back to the control.*

* *give different controls to each person, and a common point to meet at.*

RELAY ORIENTEERING

AIM
• *to provide relay atmosphere and encourage team spirit*

EQUIPMENT CHECKLIST

Relay events are fun - short courses, team work - usually a mass start - everyone together.

Preparation

Relay events take a lot of preparation but they are worth it for the enjoyment they give. Use an area with which the group is familiar.

Prepare three short courses of similar length and shape (probably 1.5 - 2km). Some controls can be common to two or all three courses. If the legs take longer than 10-15 minutes the group waiting may get bored.

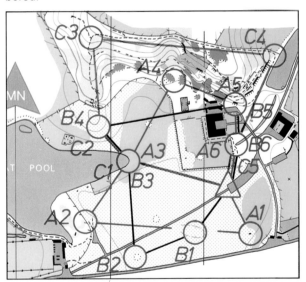

Control number	Control code
A1	XY
B1	XZ
C1 A3 B3	AB
A2	AC
B2	AD
C2 B4	AE
C3	MP
A4	HA
C4	HC
A5 B5	HG
A6 B6 C5	XX

Prepare control description lists for each course, including codes.

Prepare pre-marked maps, one set of three (courses A, B, C) for each team of three. Each person should have a control card.

Set out the course using the master map, punching three master cards, one for each course.

This example shows three relay courses using permanent controls (A-red, B-black, C-blue)
e.g. Course A:

COURSE A		
1	XY	Hut
2	AC	Path end
3	AB	Pool. E.tip
4	HA	Thicket, S.end
5	HG	Crag foot
6	XX	River, W.end

Practical

Students work in teams of three to run the three legs.

On the whistle for 'Go' all first leg runners set off on a course. This may be A, B or C, the order can be predetermined by the organiser.

When a team's first leg runner returns, they touch the second leg runner who goes out on a different course. The idea is that, by the end of the relay, all three runners have run all three courses between them.

The order is varied to prevent following - which can easily happen in a massed start. The first team to complete three legs is the winner.

For example, with six teams the leg order is:

Team 1	ABC	Team 4	BAC
Team 2	ACB	Team 5	CAB
Team 3	BCA	Team 6	CBA

This way teams are split slightly.

Note: spectator controls add to the excitement, e.g. No. 3 is visible from Start/Finish.

Adaptations and further work

(see also p28)

A relay could be made up of 2 legs only with 2 in a team. This would take less time but there would be more people going to the first controls - more than one punch would be needed at the first controls.

Head to head race. Only one course needed. Pair off the group according to ability. One of each pair goes one way and races the other who goes the opposite way. First back wins.

PAIRS ORIENTEERING

AGE GROUP   12+
TIME   30-60 min

AIM
• to encourage pupils to go out alone in a new area

EQUIPMENT CHECKLIST

Preparation

A local park would be best used if the group has always gone in pairs. Make use of a permanent course if available.

Pupils work in pairs and keep parting and meeting up at alternate controls.

Prepare a course with an alternative extra control on each leg as shown below. With novices keep the controls on line features with an obvious route. If anyone gets lost it will mean a lot of waiting around for their partner.

Control descriptions:

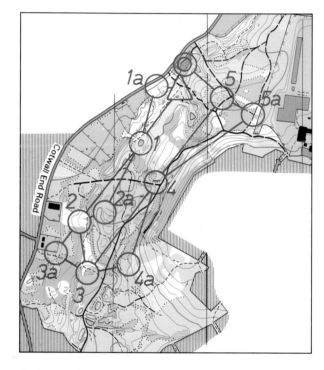

COURSE 1 (harder)		
1	AB	Pond, south side
2a	AF	Large depression, west end
2	AX	Stream bend
3	BP	Knoll
4a	BX	Foot of steep slope
4	BY	Cliff foot
5	XX	Between knolls

COURSE 2 (easier)		
1a	PS	Gully
1	AB	Pond, south side
2	AX	Stream bend
3a	BH	Path
3	BP	Knoll
4	BY	Cliff foot
5a	PH	Path junction
5	XX	Between knolls

Prepare description lists for each of the pair, taking the extra controls alternately. See above.

Set out the course and punch a master card.

Lesson

Pupils set off in pairs.

Runner 1 goes to control 1 and waits.

Runner 2 goes to controls 1a + 1 and meets runner 1.

They do this around the whole course waiting at the common controls.

Adaptations

Ideal for mixed ability groups, the weaker partner doing the short legs between common controls.

The exercise can be run twice by swapping courses.

Further work

Add more controls to the extra legs between common controls.

With no waiting at common controls it could be used as a sort of relay training for advanced runners.

Change the form of course to line, contour only, etc.

PRACTICAL INTRODUCTION TO CONTOURS

AIM
* *to introduce and increase an understanding of contours through developing the picture of the terrain from the map*

EQUIPMENT CHECKLIST
tapes, card

Preparation

Contour-only maps are much easier to use than might first appear. They simplify the information to be read off the map and enable students to focus their attention on the shape of the terrain.

A contour-only map can easily be made by tracing the contours from the area to be used. Alternatively ask the mapmaker or copyright holder for a copy of the brown tracing. Add north-south (magnetic) lines.

Computer simulation is an excellent learning tool. Look for computer software that explains contours.

Using the theory on p91, 104 and worksheet 2 (p107), plan a series of progressive lessons on understanding contours and their interpretation in orienteering navigation. Use some or all the exercises below.

MUD RELIEF MAPS

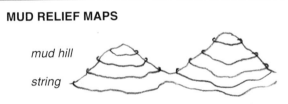

mud hill

string

A reminder of the indoor theory - using a sand tray - stone in water - cut potato.

POINT TO POINT COURSE

Put cards out at some controls to draw attention to the contours, e.g. 'is it up or down to the next control?', 'you can follow a contour line to 4 - does this mean you go up, or stay at the same height?'

Teaching checklist:
* Slopes
* Hill tops
* Depressions
* Shapes - spurs and re-entrants
* Form lines
* What is up, what is down?

* Create a mental picture from the map.
* Tell yourself what you expect to see.
* Navigate by contour features - not necessarily in a straight line.

LINE or TAPED ROUTE

Link together controls on a star exercise.

Best done in pairs.

Keep the route short, 0.5-1km

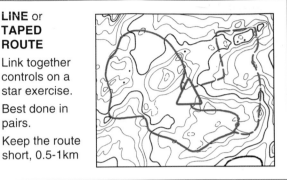

MAP WALK

Walk along a line in a group. Return via controls as individuals or pairs. Look at contour shapes on the map and the ground.

STRING COURSE

Put out tapes or string linking distinctive contour features:
* put the line on the map and identify the position of 4-6 controls.
* pupils plot the taped route on to the map. Give the start and finish.

STAR EXERCISE

Contour controls on coloured and contour-only maps. Keep legs under 200m.

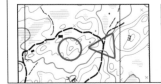

GOING TO AN EVENT

AIM

• to outline the procedures for going to an orienteering event

EQUIPMENT CHECKLIST
map case, safety pins, tape, scissors, whistle

After 3-4 school based courses pupils will benefit from going to an orienteering event. This is straightforward.

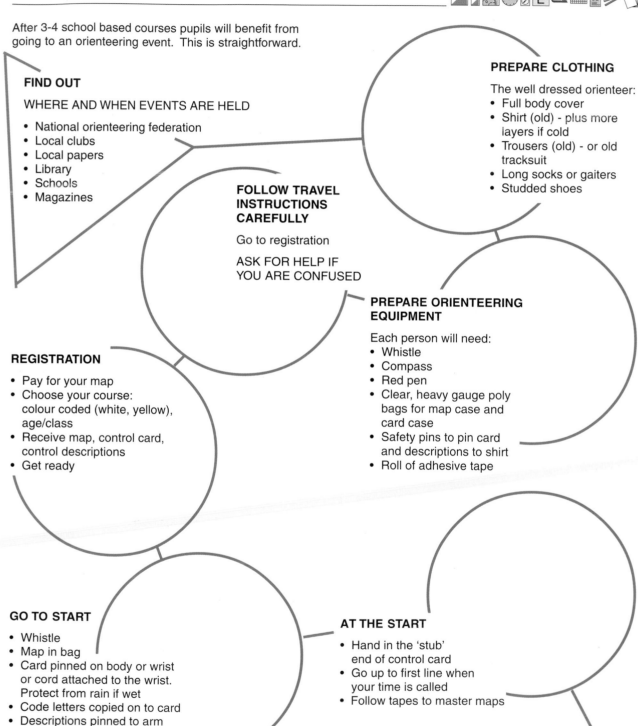

FIND OUT

WHERE AND WHEN EVENTS ARE HELD

• National orienteering federation
• Local clubs
• Local papers
• Library
• Schools
• Magazines

PREPARE CLOTHING

The well dressed orienteer:
• Full body cover
• Shirt (old) - plus more layers if cold
• Trousers (old) - or old tracksuit
• Long socks or gaiters
• Studded shoes

FOLLOW TRAVEL INSTRUCTIONS CAREFULLY

Go to registration

ASK FOR HELP IF YOU ARE CONFUSED

PREPARE ORIENTEERING EQUIPMENT

Each person will need:
• Whistle
• Compass
• Red pen
• Clear, heavy gauge poly bags for map case and card case
• Safety pins to pin card and descriptions to shirt
• Roll of adhesive tape

REGISTRATION

• Pay for your map
• Choose your course: colour coded (white, yellow), age/class
• Receive map, control card, control descriptions
• Get ready

GO TO START

• Whistle
• Map in bag
• Card pinned on body or wrist or cord attached to the wrist. Protect from rain if wet
• Code letters copied on to card
• Descriptions pinned to arm for easy reference
• Red pen at the ready

AT THE START

• Hand in the 'stub' end of control card
• Go up to first line when your time is called
• Follow tapes to master maps

GOOD LUCK

PERMANENT COURSES

AIM
• *to use permanent courses to introduce the sport of orienteering*

EQUIPMENT CHECKLIST
safety pins, whistle

Preparation

Buy maps and check the recommended courses. If the courses are not suitable for your exercise, plan new ones making use of the permanent controls but in a different order. If possible buy maps without all the controls overprinted and pre-mark them with the course you want to use.

If you use the area regularly with groups of varying ability, prepare the maps then cover them with clear matt adhesive film:

• Mark the north side very clearly with red ink.
• Trim the map so that it is as small as possible. Cut off the legend and stick it on the back.
• Mark any out-of-bounds areas or any necessary instructions, e.g. if lost follow the road downhill.
• Number each map for ease of organisation.

For extra protection put the covered map into a sealed polythene bag.

Courses can be marked on a covered map with a permanent felt-tip pen (fine point). This can be removed with methylated spirit. Use a circle template.

Prepare control cards (rainproofed), descriptions (on card or beside the course in the map unit), pencils (tie on string and safety pin to body). Try to organise the various bits and pieces of equipment so that only the map has to be held and there is no effort in reaching the control card and descriptions.

For complete beginners if the controls are not at every decision point (a change of direction or line feature) then the course is <u>not</u> easy enough.

• plan a map walk first, or
• set up a 'star' exercise to introduce map features, teach setting the map and give confidence, or
• set out more controls to make the course easier.

Have a preparation lesson looking at maps and show a short video or slides of orienteering.

Lesson

Give out a map each. Orientate the group to the surroundings and take them on a short map walk. Show them a control marker with code system. With young beginners it is best then to send them round the course you have just walked round.

Give out control cards, pencils and descriptions.

Demonstrate the advantages of pinning the card and a

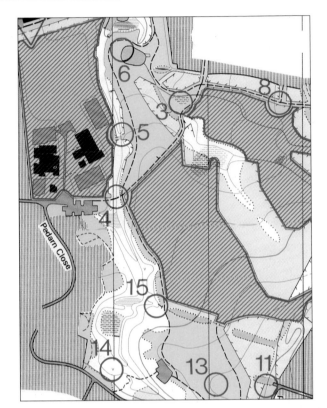

pencil to jacket or trousers - out of the way, safe, handy

String round groove in short pencil.

Open end of poly bag so that card can be written on and stay dry.

Discuss safety directions, use of whistle and give a time limit.

Time them on a course as individuals or pairs - no groups, if you want them all to learn to read the map. 2-5 minute intervals will help prevent larger groups forming.

Further work

Most of the lessons in this section can be adapted for use on a permanent course. Consider which skills you want to teach (preferably one at a time) and use the control sites to plan your exercises.

Ask your local club for a list of local permanent courses (p153).

NIGHT ORIENTEERING - INTRODUCTION

AGE GROUP 10+
TIME

AIM
* *to introduce young people to night orienteering*

EQUIPMENT CHECKLIST
torches/headlamps, whistles

Preparation

Select an area with plenty of line features and distinct boundaries. School or centre grounds offer a secure environment.

Go out and look at it in darkness.

Plan the exercise: a line + three or four controls (A-D), then a point to point course - see example. The course should use easy line features - yellow standard.

Pre-mark separate maps for
      (a) the line + three or four controls (A-D) and
      (b) for the point to point course
(each member of group will need both maps).

Lesson

Check clothing and torches/headlamps. If headlamps are used, adjust so that the beam shines on the ground about 2m ahead. If torches are used, attach them to a band on the shoulder or wrist, to leave the hands free. Check that spare batteries are carried, and a spare small torch.

Follow the line on the map as a group:

* pace counting can be reassuring. It is more useful in the dark than during the day as visibility is so much restricted. It must be practised.

* observe shapes in the dark.

* keep (and look) to the side of a line feature you want to turn off.

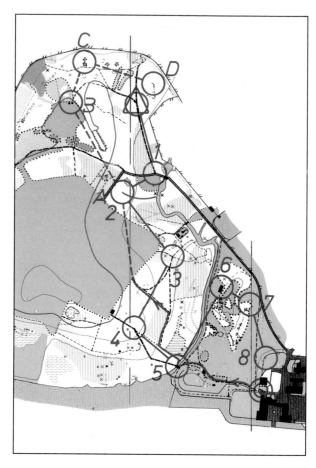

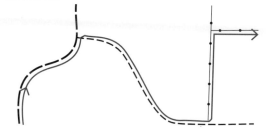

At the end of the walk (line) visit the first two controls (A, B) as a group using attack points and accurate compass work. The next two controls (C, D) should be done in pairs, assembling at the finish control/start of the point to point course.

Set the group off as individuals or pairs on the point to point course. It uses the same area that has just been walked through.

Time the point to point course as in a competition.

Adaptation

A star exercise would also be a good introduction to night orienteering. It increases confidence.

Further work

A mass start score event. Having other people around gives confidence in the dark. Visit 2 - 3 controls in a group as a warm up.

Have 3 very short loops (600 - 900m) on paths only. Use as individuals or as a relay.

NIGHT ORIENTEERING

AIMS
- *to develop night orienteering skills*
- *to increase confidence in techniques used in the daytime*

AGE GROUP	14+ pairs 12+
TIME	60-90 min

EQUIPMENT CHECKLIST
torches/headlamps, whistles, reflective tape

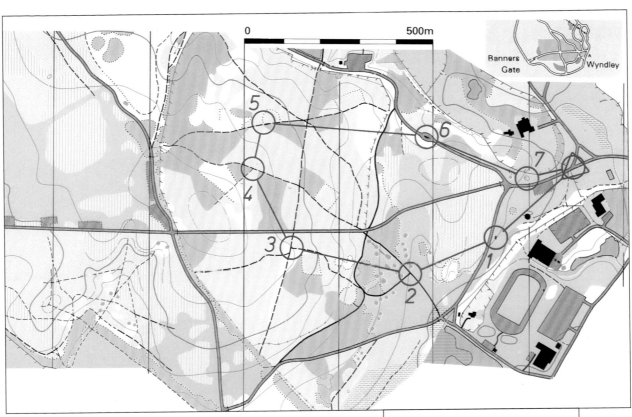

Preparation and practical

Plan a straightforward course using line features (yellow standard).

Draw master maps and prepare control descriptions.

The preparation and organisation of a night event is the same as a daytime orienteering event, except that the competition takes place in the dark.

Avoid crags and dangerous ground.

Check the course <u>at night</u> to ensure that it is not too difficult.

Reflective strips can be hung at each control to help visibility for beginners.

Set students off and time them round the course. They can go in pairs or alone.

Night events of many different types can be organised.

It is recommended that students carry a large torch <u>and</u> a spare if possible.

CONTROL DESCRIPTIONS

1	XA	Hut, N. corner
2	YB	Road junction
3	XB	N. path junction
4	YH	Path junction
5	XX	Path/edge of clearing
6	AB	Road island
7	CX	Depression

Adaptations and further work

Any type of exercise already described is possible at night, especially those in chapter 3.

Street events are possible at night (p109).

Mini-orienteering, at night - a fun event. Use punches only. Set a course in a parkland area where there is one building. The lights in the building are on but there are no lights in the parkland. Runners have to keep returning to the light to see their maps - no torches allowed. They have to feel around for the punch!

5

TECHNIQUE TRAINING

This section is designed to offer a selection of exercises and training skills required for the successful completion of more technical courses. The exercises are designed for training rather than teaching. The section is planned for students who are fairly competent in basic skills and involves route choice, more precise use of map and compass and distance judgement, e.g. orange-green standard (p132).

Woodland areas with plenty of contour detail are most suitable but parks and rough open areas can be just as useful with thoughtful planning.

Most lessons in the previous sections can be adapted and made more challenging in more complex forested or open terrain.

CORRIDOR ORIENTEERING

AIMS
• to focus attention on the straight line route choice
• to encourage pupils to follow routes without using line features as handrails

EQUIPMENT CHECKLIST

Preparation

This exercise will make a familiar area with many line features more interesting and challenging. A narrow 'corridor' between controls is all the map that is given. Navigation along the corridor will require map reading and use of compass. There will be no route choice and no option of following handrails.

Plan a route keeping legs relatively short (100-300m) and with a large or distinctive feature just before the control. Define the edges of the corridor remembering that the width of the corridor will determine the degree of difficulty of the exercise (wider = easier).

Prepare maps either by cutting out or by opaquing the area of map not to be shown. Pupils could prepare their own but it is better if they do not see the map outside the corridor. If maps have to be reused, cut out and attach blank paper to cover the areas not required.

Prepare a control description list as the example below.

Set out the control markers and punch a master card.

Decide on the best relocation direction.

The corridor must be tested for reliability of the map and runnability of the terrain (nettles, brambles, etc.)

Practical

Brief the group on the purpose of the exercise.

Tell them how to relocate themselves if lost.

Set pupils off on the course at 1-2 minute intervals (individually or in pairs).

Time their return and calculate times taken.

Adaptations

The corridor can be made wider or narrower according to the ability of the class.

Contour-only maps can be used if there is sufficient detail for navigation.

Further work

Window orienteering (p56).

Point to point courses with straight line route choice possibilities - but start with short easy legs.

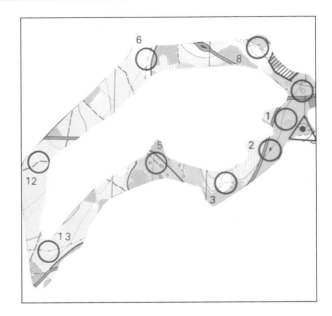

Control descriptions

1	1	Thicket, N. side
2	2	Building, S. side
3	3	Re-entrant
4	5	Gully
5	13	Small earth wall
6	12	Path bend
7	6	Fence
8	8	Fence corner
9	9	Depression

WINDOW ORIENTEERING

AIM

• to test distance estimation, and relocation within the 'window'

EQUIPMENT CHECKLIST

This could be used in a very familiar area to make the exercise more difficult.

Preparation

This exercise is similar to corridor orienteering but now only a window around the control is shown. Pupils must use a compass and estimate distance to reach the window, then relocate on the detail in the window before finding the control.

When planning the course make sure that each window contains sufficient good detail for relocation. The size of the window will determine the degree of difficulty of the exercise (larger = easier).

Prepare maps by opaquing the area of map not to be shown. Pupils could prepare their own but it is better if they do not see the map outside the corridor. If maps have to be reused, cut out and attach blank paper to cover the areas not required.

Prepare a control description list.

Set out the course and punch a master card.

Decide on the best relocation direction.

The route must be tested for reliability of the map and runnability of the terrain (nettles, brambles, etc.)

The course can be planned to increase in difficulty, starting as a corridor then using large windows on line features - slowly decreasing their size.

Practical

Explain the purpose of the exercise to the group.

Check that they can all take a compass bearing and know how many paces they take for 100m.

Remind them of the map scale.

Tell them how to relocate themselves if lost.

Set pupils off on the course at 1-2 minute intervals.

Time their return and calculate times taken.

Adaptations

The course can be made easier by having taped routes between the windows. Pupils follow the route and when they reach the end of the tape they must locate their position in the window.

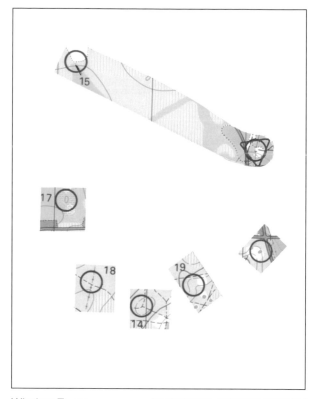

Window Event
Master Map
- using mainly
permanent
controls

		Control descriptions
1	15	Wood, S. end
2	17	Knoll, E. side
3	18	Small earth wall
4	14	Path junction
5	19	Re-entrant
6	-	Thicket, E. side

Alternatively instructions could be given on how to get from one window to another, e.g. follow road south 300m.

Further work

The course can be made harder by decreasing the size of the windows and/or increasing the distance between them.

NORWEGIAN EVENT AND MAP MEMORY

AIMS
* *the Norwegian event is similar to point to point orienteering*
* *(in the map memory exercise) to hold in the mind the major features on each leg and the map around the control site*

EQUIPMENT CHECKLIST

This exercise is so-called as it was introduced to Britain by Norwegian orienteers. It is a useful way of planning longer courses in a small area. Such a course can cross back over itself numerous times. If the whole course were given at the start the fastest route would be to take controls out of order. The preparation is similar for both exercises.

Preparation

NORWEGIAN EVENT

Prepare a point to point course on a map and keep this as your master.

Prepare sections of map just showing 2 controls e.g. 1-2, 2-3, 3-4 etc. (see right). Highlight north on the map.

Stick each section on a separate card, and protect it if necessary. Punch a hole in the top of the card and attach string for hanging at each control.

Set out the course. At the start hang the map section showing the start to control 1. At control 1 leave the section from control 1 to control 2, etc. Remember to punch a master card.

Prepare a control description list.

Practical

Each pupil has a blank map. When it is their start time they copy the start and control 1 on to their map and set off. When they reach control 1 they will find the map with leg 1 - 2 on it. They punch their card, copy control 2 and set off to control 2. And so on.

Adaptation

MAP MEMORY

For this exercise the preparation is exactly the same as the Norwegian event. However map memory can also be introduced with a star exercise (see p42).

*In this exercise **pupils do not have a map**. At the start they look at the map section provided and **memorise** a route to control 1. Here they punch their card and memorise the route to control 2, etc.*

To start with, keep route choice and navigation simple and legs under 400m. If they do not find a control they must find their way back to the last one and try again. Give a safety bearing to return to the finish if lost.

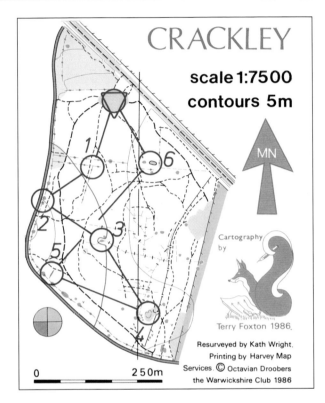

CRACKLEY

scale 1:7500
contours 5m

MN

Cartography by

Terry Foxton 1986.

Resurveyed by Kath Wright.
Printing by Harvey Map
Services © Octavian Droobers
the Warwickshire Club 1986

0   250m

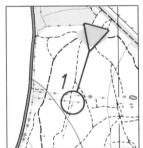
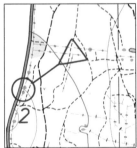

Further work

Exercises can be made more difficult by planning a more difficult course.

It is useful to get pupils to try to draw their course on a blank map after a memory course.

Map memory score event - one master map at the base, visit as many controls as possible by memory.

Star exercise - one, two or three controls memorised.

Control picking and traffic light orienteering - practice visualising and memorising attack point to control.

TRAFFIC LIGHT ORIENTEERING

AGE GROUP 12+
TIME 60-120 min

AIMS
- *to encourage students to slow down as they approach controls*
- *to practise the idea of rough and fine orienteering*
- *to practise using attack points*
- *to establish a disciplined approach to route execution*

EQUIPMENT CHECKLIST

Preparation

Plan a 2-3 km point to point course with good attack points before the controls.

Prepare a master map. Draw the route to be followed in green, amber and red to indicate fast, medium and slow sections.

Master map

▬▬▬ Green - fast sections

▬▬▬ Amber - slowing down

☐ Red - attack point

Slow into control

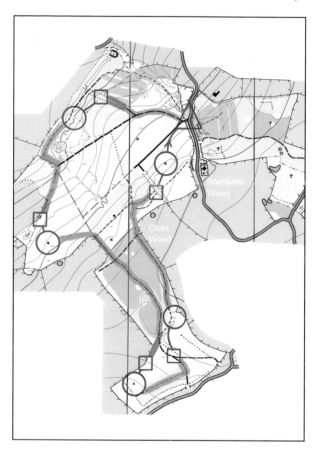

In green sections rough orienteering is required and speed can be fast. In the amber and red sections speed must be reduced as fine orienteering is required to locate the attack point and read the map into the control.

Use red squares to indicate possible attack points. Note that an attack point can be at the start or finish of an amber section, or both, depending upon its size and the difficulty of the control (see theory chapter p87).

Set out the course and punch a master card.

Prepare control descriptions and codes.

Practical

This is a training exercise. Explain the purpose of the traffic light idea. Send pupils out at 1-2 min intervals.

Adaptations and further work

Pupils can decide their own fast and slow sections.

This exercise can be used with those relating to compass work, distance judgement and control picking.

Traffic light orienteering can be used as a star exercise.

The controls could just be marked with tape instead of markers for more experienced groups.

Divide each leg into two parts. The first part is a corridor for rough orienteering, the second part is a 'line' leading into the control demanding detailed map reading and fine orienteering. Encourage adjustment of speed in competition.

Control descriptions:

1 AB Re-entrant
2 AC Boulder, S. side
3 AD Pile of stones
4 EB Depression
5 EC Pile of stones

PIECE OF CAKE (HANGING CONTROLS)

AIM
• to improve confidence in fine map reading by control site identification

EQUIPMENT CHECKLIST

Preparation

Finding a feature and hanging a control flag is a much more advanced skill than finding a control in competition. Groups should be asked to do this in pairs at first, especially if they are inexperienced (orange standard or less). The principle is very similar to a star exercise.

Prepare a master map and divide it into sections as shown - each section having two controls which will be put out by one pair. The control sites should suit the ability of the pair in question.

Prepare a separate map and control descriptions for each section.

e.g.   Section A

        Path bend

        Re-entrant

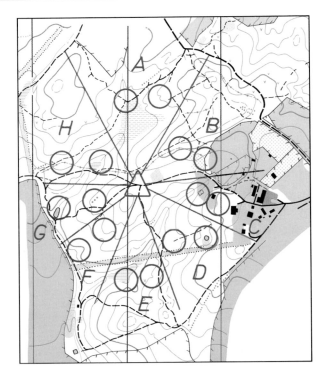

Practical

Students work in pairs. They can put the controls out together or one control each.

Everyone must return to the base once they have hung the controls.

Pairs then swap maps and go out to find controls in other sections, as pairs or as individuals.

OR

The whole group can go around all the controls to discuss how well they are placed

> - on the right feature?
> - too high?
> - too low? . . . etc.

Pairs are sent to bring in controls when the exercise is finished.

Although this exercise is a good way of using an area with which pupils are familiar, it is most beneficial in a new area.

Adaptations and further work

The control sites could be premarked with yellow tape and a number to help identify sites.

Students could select their own control sites within their section.

Self perpetuating course (p66).

MIXTURE EXERCISES

AIMS
- *to improve concentration whilst switching from one exercise to another*
- *to maintain interest and motivation over a longer period of time when one exercise could become boring*
- *to give further practice of techniques already introduced and practised singly*

EQUIPMENT CHECKLIST

Preparation and practical

The exercise consists of:

1 SCORE EVENT
   Take controls A - F in any order, finish at G (10 points for each control).

2 LINE ORIENTEERING (p40)
   Three control sites to be identified on the map.

3 CORRIDOR ORIENTEERING (p55)

4 WINDOW ORIENTEERING (p56)

5 NORWEGIAN OR MAP MEMORY EVENT (p57)

Not as complex as it may look - this is merely a mixture of some of the previous exercises.

Prepare a clear master map. Remember that the 3 controls in the line orienteering section are not shown on the master map

Prepare separate master map sections to hang at each control for the Norwegian/map memory part. Cut away this section of the main master map.

Remember to punch a master card when setting out the course.

Adaptations and further work

There are many possible combinations of exercises. They should be kept relatively short.

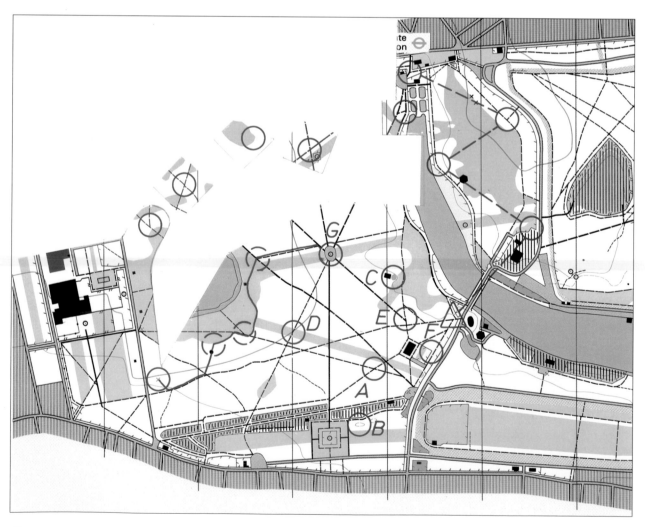

'ALL IN' 2 COURSE RELAY

AIM
• *to provide relay excitement with very little organisation*

EQUIPMENT CHECKLIST

Preparation

This relay is planned for teams of three and is ideal for mixed ability teams. It requires 2 courses. As in most relays, controls should be easy and the length should be kept under 2km.

Plan two courses of similar length and difficulty and draw a master map for reference.

Prepare two maps for each team of 3 - one of each course - using code letters to differentiate the courses.

Set out the controls, hanging the correct code letter at each and punching a master card for checking purposes.

A mass start simplifies the organisation and makes it more fun. A third of the group (one from each team) will be running the first course together. Another third will be running the second course. The remainder will be waiting for the first runners back before starting. Two punches should be used at the first controls on each course to avoid queuing.

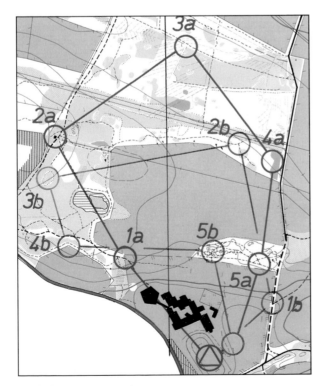

Red circles - course A
Blue circles - course B
Start and finish at the running track

Practical

Two members of each team will be running at the same time - one on course A, one on course B. It is best to send a fast and slow person out to start with.

Team   Runner 1 (fast)

Runner 2 (medium)

Runner 3 (slow)

The first one back hands the map to the 3rd runner, the second one back hands the map to the first one back and so on until all 3 team members have run both courses:

START

Runner 1 takes course A

Runner 2 takes course B

Runner 1 returns - runner 2 takes course B

Runner 3 returns - runner 1 takes course B

Runner 2 returns - runner 3 takes course A

Runner 1 returns - runner 2 takes course B

Runner 3 returns

Runner 2 returns

FINISH!

Course A	Course B
1 Gate	1 Track junction
2 Building, N. side	2 Path junction
3 Fence end	3 Clearing
4 Thicket corner	4 Fence corner
5 Path junction	5 Hill top

Adaptations and further work

Longer courses can be used for training purposes.

Less able runners could work in pairs.

With a large group start teams at 30 second intervals or plan four courses to split the runners up and discourage following. All three members of each team should still complete the same two courses.

One-on-one relay with one course and pairs of equal ability. A starts clockwise, B anticlockwise and the first back wins. Plan the course to be as equal as possible in either direction.

PUZZLE ORIENTEERING

AIMS
* *to provide variety - a fun event*
* *to mix theory with practical*

EQUIPMENT CHECKLIST
tapes, jigsaws +

Preparation

In puzzle orienteering anything goes! Pupils should have some theoretical knowledge, e.g. bearings, pacing, map symbols etc.

The principle is like a 'Norwegian' event. Runners find out at each control where to go next. To find this out they have to complete certain tasks. Instructions for these are on prepared cards set out at the control.

Preparation depends on the course planner. This example is just for guidance and ideas.

Practical

START: pupils have to complete a map jigsaw before they can look at the start card.

CARDS: put the start card at the start, card 1 at control 1, etc.

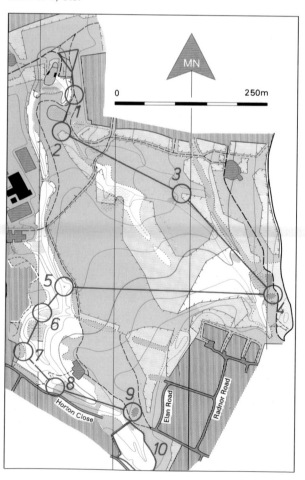

Start Follow path south until you see no. 1!

1 Follow bearing 190° to no. 2. Count paces!

3 No. 4 is a thicket (east side) some-where in this square of map.

2 How far have you come since no. 1?
Multi-choice answer
(a) 130m (b) 200m (c) 250m
If your answer is (a) go to 3a, (b) go to 3b, (c) go to 3c.
There is a control marker only at the correct place.

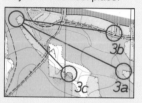

4 No. 5 is a small pit in this area of map.

5 No. 6 is a marsh 100m from here - there are several marshes, you have to guess!

6 Follow tapes to no. 7 - beware, it is not that easy.

7 Where are you now?
If you answer 7a, no.8 is a car park.
If 7b, no. 8 is along the road to the east end.
If 7c, no. 8 is along the road to the second clearing.

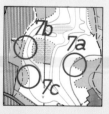

8 Which symbol represents a large depression,
(a) ⊖ (b) ∨ (c) o ?
If (a), go to 9a.
If (b), go to 9b.
If (c), go to 9c.

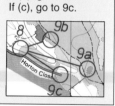

9 Control 10 is wandering in this area of the map! You have to find it before finishing.

Adaptations and further work

There are many possibilities! The multi-choice answer can include many subjects. ('What is the name of the local orienteering club?', etc.) Some controls could be punches only, some could have physical tasks - rope swing, swim (in summer), etc.

MIXED ABILITY COURSES

AIM
* *to allow mixed ability groups to run a point to point course with the minimum amount of course planning and hanging controls*

EQUIPMENT CHECKLIST

Preparation

Plan a course where controls have distinct easy features in front of them to use as attack points. Prepare three different master maps.

The first master map shows only the attack points - 1a, 2a, 3a, etc. (control markers used).

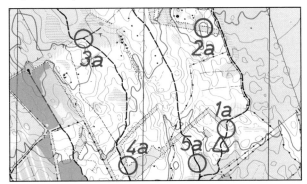

The second master map shows attack points plus controls, marked with tapes only.

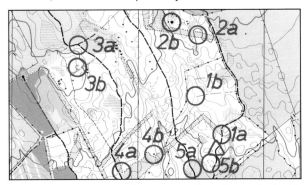

The third master map shows controls only, marked with tapes - 1b, 2b, 3b etc.

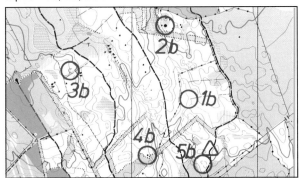

Set out the course with markers and codes at the attack points, and just tapes at the controls

Practical

The class is split into 3 ability groups.

The least able run the course using map 1, finding controls 1a, 2a, 3a, etc.

The middle group runs the course using map 2, finding first attack points 1a, 2a, etc. and using them to navigate slowly into the taped controls 1b, 2b, etc.

The most able group runs a point to point course using map 3, finding only the taped controls 1b, 2b, etc. They know nothing about the controls hanging at the attack points.

Adaptations and further work

Mini controls may be hung instead of tape.

RELOCATION IN PAIRS

AIMS
- *to enable students to practise the valuable skill of relocation*
- *to allow pupils to run in pairs learning from each other*

EQUIPMENT CHECKLIST

Preparation

This is minimal. Just set a course and put markers out. No punches are needed as this is a non-competitive training exercise. Code letters are useful but not a necessity - omitting them makes it more difficult.

Examples of attack points can be shown for the first two controls - the attack points must be within 50-100m of the control. Marking an area of 200m diameter round each control directs the leader into the right area to select an attack point and facilitates the relocation process. This is good for developing confidence in a skill which is so often affected by panic and anxiety.

Prepare one map for each pair with controls, attack points and 200m circles as necessary.

Practical

Students set off in pairs with one map between two. The one leading has the map and runs to an attack point.

At the attack point runner 1 hands the map to runner 2 who must relocate and then find the control. Runner 2 then continues to an attack point for control 2, and so on.

Adaptations and other work

There does not have to be a course set out. Runner 1 could run to any point and hand the map to runner 2.

*Alternatively the **following** runner could carry the map and the first runner without a map can go anywhere. They will be running faster and so the following runner will be practising 'retrospective' navigation at speed.*

Runners should be encouraged to stop every few minutes and discuss the route on the map. With a mixed ability pair the stronger orienteer can spot the other's mistakes and help.

The teacher could lead the group through the terrain. After a distance of 300-500 metres, maps are given out and the group members have to draw the route they have taken. The exercise can be repeated with the distance gradually increased. This could also be done in pairs. It helps to answer the question 'which way have I come?'.

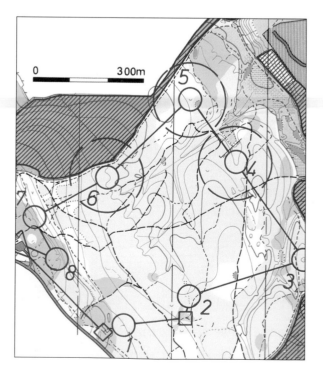

Control Descriptions

1 Gully
2 Ditch bend
3 Depression
4 Re-entrant
5 Depression
6 Spur
7 Re-entrant
8 Re-entrant

RELOCATION - FOLLOW MY LEADER

AGE GROUP	14+
TIME	60 min

AIM

• *to try to "lose" the group and therefore give them practice at relocation*

EQUIPMENT CHECKLIST

Preparation

Use an area with distinctive features to relocate on. Prepare a master map of a course in a small area (with 10 controls for 10 students, 11 controls for 11 students, etc.).

Prepare a map for each control, each map showing one control only. Write the code and description on each map.

Put controls out.

Students prepare control cards writing codes in the boxes. They must all have a different control for no. 1 and then for no. 2, etc.

4 students (A, B, C, D)

control	A	B	C	D
1	AB	AC	AD	AE
2	AC	AD	AE	AF
3	AD	AE	AF	BB

Leader's Master Map

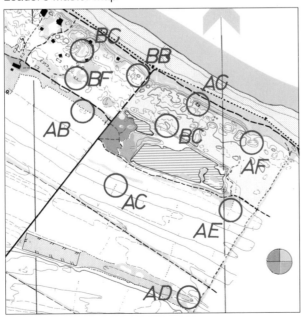

Practical

Discuss skills and drills of relocation:

a) developing terrain memory

b) finding a definite point on a line feature if immediate relocation is not possible.

Brief everyone on the procedure of the exercise.

The leader (teacher) runs through the area carrying all the maps. Pupils follow trying to remember features they pass.

The leader stops at a definite point and hands out maps to students, i.e. student A gets map AB, and so on.

They 'relocate' and run off to find the control, punch their cards, and return to the stopping place.

When everyone has returned they proceed as before.

You can do as many controls as you wish, see below.

Students have to remember where they were 'dropped off' to be able to return there.

Adaptations and further work

Marking all controls on each map the leader can stop at a control anywhere then all meet up at another specified control. Alternatively individuals are given one control to find, then asked to meet up at a common control e.g. go to 6 then meet up at 4.

The exercise can be made harder, using contour-only maps, for example.

It could be used to practise bearings - taking a bearing from control to relocation point and following it.

SELF PERPETUATING COURSE

AIMS
- *to allow a training course to run itself*
- *to provide a 'catch me' chasing opportunity*
- *to increase confidence by locating a feature to hang the control*
- *to develop the skills of orienteering at speed*

EQUIPMENT CHECKLIST

Preparation

This exercise needs minimal preparation as the group puts the controls out.

Plan a course with as many controls as students in the group, e.g. 8. Place the start centrally.

Make one or two master maps.

The control sites should be selected according to the standard of the group but all controls should be on very distinctive features to give the group confidence in hanging controls at the correct sites.

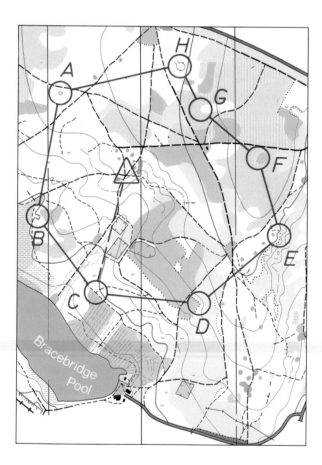

Practical

The group copies the course on to their maps.

Each pupil is allocated a control and they go from the start to that control point (i.e. each to a different one) and hang a marker there. They then continue around the course in the order shown - the runner that hangs a control at C then goes to D, E, F, G, H, A, B, C in that order. They finish at the control they put out and bring it back to the start. In this way there is no putting out of controls for the teacher.

Control descriptions

A Knoll
B Re-entrant
C Path junction
D Thicket corner
E Re-entrant
F Thicket, W. edge
G Copse, W. end
H Inside earth wall

Adaptations and further work

The exercise can be made harder by using more technical control sites.

It can be made easier by using easy control points and with the children working in pairs.

Short legs demand continuous map contact and concentration, long legs introduce route choice and rough orienteering.

SURPRISE MAP DRAWING

AIM
• to test terrain memory by making students describe and draw a route

EQUIPMENT CHECKLIST

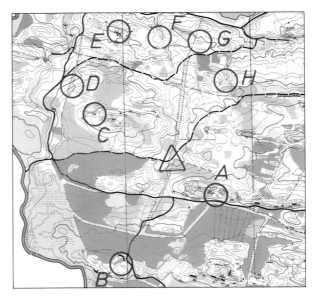

Preparation

Minimal preparation is required.

Plan a starting point and as many controls as pupils in the group. Bear in mind that navigation to all controls will be from the starting point.

Prepare a master map for each student, putting the start and one control on each map.

Remember to take pencils and paper.

Practical

Go to the central starting place. Give each student a map (but only let them see the position of their own control).

Each student visits their control site, hangs a marker there and returns to the start.

THEN SURPRISE THEM!

They expect just to swap maps with someone and then go off to the control .... but ....

Collect the maps.

Give paper and a pencil to each student. They have to draw a map to enable someone else to find the control. No conferring is allowed. They have to find and collect controls using the sketch maps.

Vary the numbers of colours allowed for drawing. Vary the annotations allowed.

Some examples of what may be drawn:

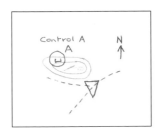

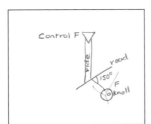

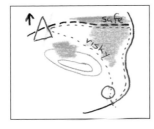

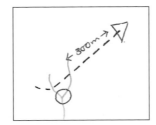

Adaptations

To make it easier, let them look at a course map when they draw their own.

To make it harder, do not allow any annotations.

Runners can swap sketch maps and try other controls.

They could repeat the exercise - note the difference in the sketch maps when they know they will have to draw one!

Further work

Ideal training for the brain: try to draw how you got around a whole course just after finishing - without another look at the map - with another look at the map.

Games involving map drawing (p99).

1 In pairs: send them all out for 100-300m in different directions. On stopping each one draws a map of the surrounding area, hangs a control, marks it on their map and returns. They exchange maps with their partners and collect the control using their partner's map. Using line features and minimum distances from base will make it easier.

2 A short course or star exercise: blank out (liquid paper) control circles. Hang controls. Students must navigate to the centre of the circle and draw the feature(s) on which the control is hung, either on the map or in control card boxes.

'SARDINES' FUN ORIENTEERING

AIM
• to improve confidence in feature identification

AGE GROUP	15+
TIME	45-60 min

EQUIPMENT CHECKLIST

Preparation

Any area can be used for this exercise but it is better if there is plenty of detail on the map.

Select 4 - 6 areas on the map each of which has at least three examples of the same feature,

e.g.   area 1: re-entrants,

          area 2: slow run thickets,

          area 3: hill tops,

          area 4: cliffs.

The areas should be a maximum of 300 metres across. Draw them on the maps. No controls are required.

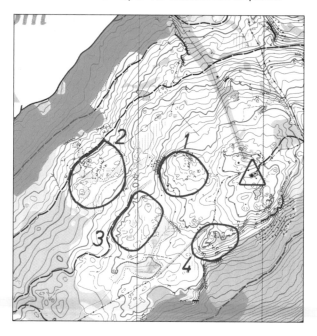

searching, all the sardines stand up and shout. They then all go off to search for the hiding place in area 2. This time it will be in a patch of slow run thicket.

Practical

Give out maps and explain the game.

One person in the group has 3 minutes to go off and hide at one of the predetermined features (re-entrant) in area 1 - it's their choice.

The rest of the group go and look for the hiding place.

The first one to find the hiding place goes off to hide in area 2. When the others find the hiding place, they stay there until everyone is together - like 'sardines'!

If, after 10 minutes, one or more of the group is still

Further fun orienteering

Knoll bagging competition - a control hung on every knoll in a defined area, no circles marked on the map. How many can you find in one hour?

Puzzle orienteering (p62).

DEVELOPING CONTOUR PERCEPTION

AGE GROUP	12+
TIME	30-60 min

AIM
* *to develop the interpretation of contour lines as an aid to map contact and route choice*

EQUIPMENT CHECKLIST

The instant interpretation of contour shapes is the art of the skilled orienteer. The first step is to recognise steep slopes, gentle slopes, distinct hill tops and know whether the going is up or down. Then progress can be made towards developing the finer interpretation of shapes and maintaining map contact when taking routes through the terrain.

In areas with contour detail but lots of line features the use of contour-only maps concentrates attention on the ground shapes, encouraging perception of the three dimensional picture. This work is the key to orienteering successfully once the beginner has progressed to more technical courses.

When using contour-only maps with juniors, add the line features around the boundary of the area. This will prevent anxiety about getting completely lost.

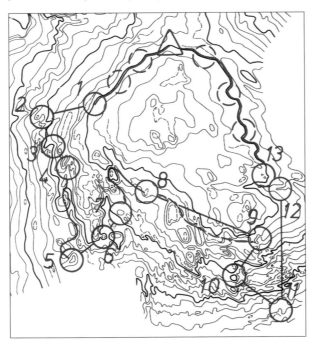

A contour-only map showing a variety of work for developing contour perception.

Preparation

The simplest way of obtaining contour-only maps is to borrow the brown film positive from the map drawer and seek permission to photocopy it. When a map is being printed it is possible to ask for copies of any single colour or combinations of colours e.g. brown,

brown + blue. As a last resort contours can be traced from a map (but there are copyright implications).

Remember to add MAGNETIC NORTH lines and SCALE to the map.

Practical

SOME APPROACHES USING CONTOUR-ONLY MAPS

1 **Contouring**. Follow a contour counting the number of mini controls you find. Stay on the same level to find all the controls.

2 **Control 'picking'** (see p80). Plan controls close together with distinct contour detail on each leg, e.g. 2-4, 5-7. This is one of the best ways of introducing contour-only maps and for developing the mental map picture from attack point to control.

3 **Lines**. Aim to keep contact with the map, memorising the main features ahead to help continuous movement. Lines should be kept short, under 500 metres, e.g. 4-5, 7-8.

4 **Slalom**. This is control picking downhill, e.g. 9-11.

5 **Longer legs**. Encourage navigation by the distinct contour features rather than by just going straight, e.g. 8-9. Long easy controls to encourage increase of speed using large contour features as collecting features, e.g. 11-12.

Further work

Corridor orienteering (p55).

Putting out controls on contour features e.g. piece of cake (p59).

Map memory - short detailed legs (p57).

Mapping very small areas.

Memory games (p97) - drawing contour pictures.

Window orienteering with distinct contour detail (p56).

6

COMPASS

Read all the way through the following pages on compass theory and practical exercises.

Plan alternate theory and practical lessons using the theory stages as a guide.

Start by identifying the parts of a compass using a large demonstration model or the blackboard. Lots of practice (15-30 times) is needed at each stage for full understanding. Each member of the group should have a compass, as sharing is impractical for effective learning.

Progressions will be found under the 'adaptations and further work' sections of each practical session.

COMPASSES FOR ORIENTEERS

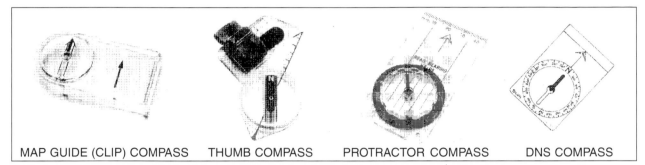

| MAP GUIDE (CLIP) COMPASS | THUMB COMPASS | PROTRACTOR COMPASS | DNS COMPASS |

The compass is a direction finding instrument, invaluable as an **aid** to precise navigation. Its skilful use will allow the orienteer to keep the map orientated, to select more direct routes and follow them faster while maintaining contact with the map.

The relationship between grid, true and magnetic north is complex and is of no great concern to orienteers. Maps for orienteering have magnetic north lines only. This simplifies map orientation or taking bearings.

The right time to introduce the compass for orienteering will always be a subject for debate. Whenever you decide to hand out the compasses, remember that the orienteering map itself takes time to understand, even for adults familiar with Ordnance Survey, USGS or other official maps. Adding the multiple complexities of a protractor compass too early in the introductory process may lead to bewilderment but will almost certainly detract attention from the MAP itself.

Courses for under 12's - in Britain the 'white' and 'yellow' colour coded courses - are planned so that a compass is not required provided that setting, or orientating, the map by the ground is understood.

We would recommend that the *protractor* compass is only introduced when the beginner is familiar with and understands:

- the map legend
- setting (orientating) the map in relation to the ground
- holding, folding and thumbing an orientated map
- route choice decisions in answer to 'What do I follow?' and 'Which way should I choose to go?'

The introduction of the *thumb* compass and the *map guide* compass allows the beginner to focus easily on the magnetic needle, quickly linking map North with magnetic North and so facilitating correct orientation of the map. This can be particularly helpful when introductory sessions take place in parks or woodland.

The *map guide* compass is recommended for young children to help them become familiar with a compass needle. This will ease the conversion to using a protractor compass later on. It also enables the child to concentrate on looking at and thumbing the MAP once it is orientated.

Thumb compasses, whilst ideal for older beginners, can be an encumbrance for very young children. Their small hands are needed primarily to hold the map. Holding map and compass together as a single unit helps to focus attention on the map. However it is less accurate than a protractor compass when moving fast along a precise line through areas of lower visibility.

The Silva DNS compass has recently been developed. This is a simplified protractor compass which can be used for introducing the compass as an alternative to the map-guide compass.

PARTS OF THE PROTRACTOR COMPASS

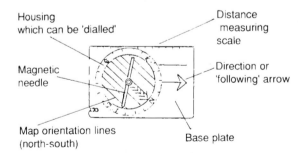

Housing which can be 'dialled'

Magnetic needle

Map orientation lines (north-south)

Distance measuring scale

Direction or 'following' arrow

Base plate

ATTACHMENT

For wrist attachment cord should be long enough to allow the compass to be turned around on the map, but short enough to allow fingers to catch the compass if dropped.

With a group it is safer to have the compasses on long neck loops. Whistles should be carried on a separate neck loop or tied where they cannot interfere with using the compass.

USING A COMPASS TO SET THE MAP

AIM
* to introduce and establish the advantages of using a compass
  to 'set' or orientate the map

EQUIPMENT CHECKLIST

STEP 1 Establish NORTH. The magnetic needle always points north-south (usually red to north). Whichever direction you face, however you twist or turn, the compass needle always points to north.

STEP 2 Fold the map small enough to 'thumb' your location. Hold the map so that you are looking straight along the route you want to take.

MAP GUIDE

STEP 3 MAP GUIDE Hold the map steady using two hands to 'steer'.

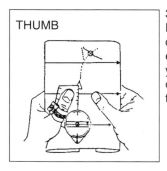

THUMB

3 THUMB Place your thumb and the corner of the leading edge of the compass at your location. Use the other hand to help hold the map steady at first.

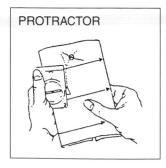

PROTRACTOR

3 PROTRACTOR Place the edge of the compass alongside the *route you want to take*. Use two hands to hold the map steady at first.

STEP 4 Turn yourself with map and compass held together in front of you until the magnetic needle of the compass lies parallel to north-south lines on the map. Needle north then equals map north.

STEP 5 You are now facing along the direction line you want to take. Take the spare hand away from the map and off you go! The protractor compass can be held in the opposite hand to the map if preferred.

STEP 6 Continue to read the map keeping your thumb at your new location. When the path changes direction, turn the map so that you are looking straight along the line you want to take - always check that needle north still points to map north.

MAP GUIDE

Practise these stages using the practical exercises 'orientation of a plan' and 'moving with map and compass' (p75,76,77) until they are fully understood before moving on to 'cutting corners'.

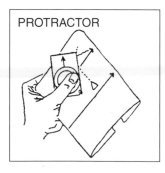

THUMB

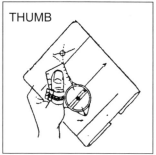

PROTRACTOR

POINTS TO WATCH

Always keep map and compass horizontal to allow the needle to swing freely.

Hold map and compass about waist level.

This is a KEY learning activity for beginners, so make sure it is not rushed. If necessary repeat it until fully understood.

CUTTING CORNERS/LOCATING ISOLATED FEATURES

AIM

• to establish good practice in progressive use of the compass

AGE GROUP

TIME

EQUIPMENT CHECKLIST

Using a map with good examples demonstrate and practise how to cut across corners and then locate isolated features.

CUTTING CORNERS

1 Is your thumb where you are?

2 Are you holding the map so that you are looking straight along the line you want to take?

3 Is the needle north pointing to map north?

4 What are you looking for? (How far is it?)

5 Off you go - read the map.

6 When you reach the wall move your thumb and reset the map.

(right) Two hands can still be used to 'steer' you through the forest.

(below) When cutting across country the leading edge of the thumb compass is placed along the line of travel, so that the thumb is beside WHERE YOU ARE GOING, not where you are.

(below right) The dial does not have to be turned - just use the needle.

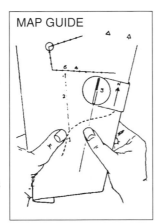

MAP GUIDE

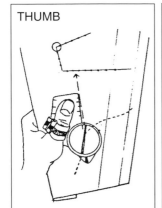

THUMB

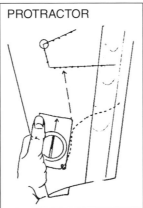

PROTRACTOR

Practise using 'rough orienteering and aiming off' (p79) and do courses with route choice options of cutting corners.

LOCATING A LARGE FEATURE OFF A LINE FEATURE

e.g. marsh, clearing, large cliff, hilltop.

Follow the same procedure as cutting a corner but be even more careful. Measure the distance.

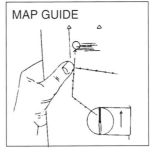

MAP GUIDE

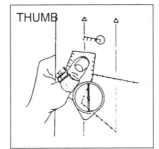

THUMB

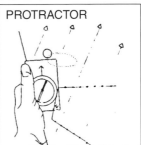

PROTRACTOR

LOCATING A SMALL FEATURE OFF A LINE FEATURE

e.g. boulder or knoll.

The same procedure as cutting corners but be very accurate and MEASURE DISTANCE PRECISELY.

MAP GUIDE

THUMB

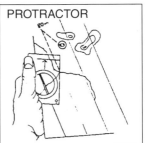

PROTRACTOR

Practise with maps in the classroom then specially planned exercises such as 'attack points' (p42) and 'traffic light orienteering' (p58).

TAKING A BEARING FROM THE MAP

AIM
* *to teach taking a compass bearing as a selective skill to be used as an aid to accurate navigation along a chosen route*

EQUIPMENT CHECKLIST

This is a natural progression from setting the map with the protractor compass and is used to obtain a more precise direction. It should always be done with care and as accurately as possible.

Follow steps 1-4 as listed on the right.

USING THE COMPASS

Premark a course on some maps and show the group different situations where you might use a compass.

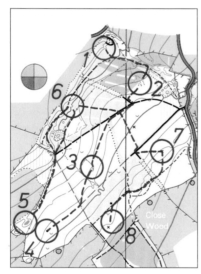

1-2

Which way do I leave this control?

Use needle or take a bearing.

2-3

Which track am I on?

Set the map.

3-4

Attack point to control.

Take a bearing.

4-5

Direct from control to control.

Take a bearing.

5-6

Measure distance along bank or path.

Use scale.

6-7

Cutting across a corner of forest and aiming off to junction.

Run on needle (rough orienteering) or take a bearing.

7-8

Is this the path on the map?

Take a bearing along the path.

I'm completely lost and want to go home!

Safety bearing east to the road.

1 Place the edge of the compass along the line you want to follow e.g. attack point-control.

Note: either edge of the base plate can be used or one of the red lines on the base plate parallel with the edge.

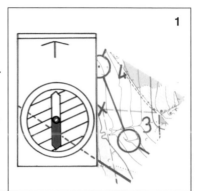

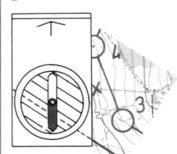

2 Turn the dial so that north on the dial points to map north - check that the lines in the housing are parallel with the north-south lines on the map.

IGNORE the magnetic needle.

3 Hold the compass LEVEL with the direction of travel arrow pointing AWAY from you.

Turn yourself until the magnetic needle lies parallel to the north-south lines in the housing.

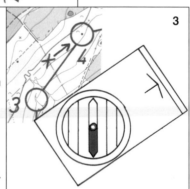

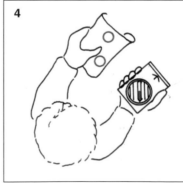

4 Follow the direction of travel arrow, READING THE MAP as well, e.g. contour 100 metres to boulder.

Look ahead and KEEP CHECKING that the needle and north-south lines in the housing are lying parallel.

ORIENTATION OF A PLAN

AIM
• to teach setting the map using the compass

EQUIPMENT CHECKLIST
ropes, benches, etc. +

Preparation

For this exercise it is best to use a large scale plan of the school field with temporary objects for features.

The plan must have magnetic north lines drawn on it.

Practical

Part 1

Lay out the temporary objects on the ground and draw them on the plan - making sure that north on the plan corresponds to north on the ground.

The pupils have to orientate (set) the plan according to the features laid out. They can check the orientation by making sure that the north lines on the plan are going the same way as the magnetic needle of the compass.

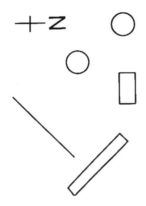

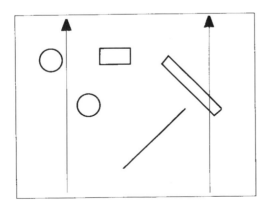

To set this plan using the objects it is necessary to turn it 90° clockwise.

Part 2

The teacher lays temporary objects down in a symmetrical pattern and draws them on to the plan. Make sure that north on the map corresponds to north on the ground (as indicated by compass).

Pupils try to orientate the plan using the features only. They realise that the plan 'fits' several ways and therefore understand the need to use the compass.

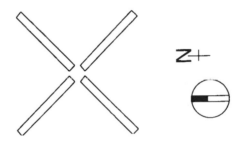

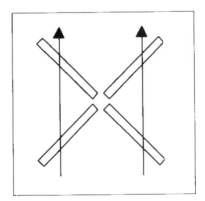

Using only objects this plan can be set 4 ways. The compass is used to set the plan in the correct direction.

The plan needs to be turned clockwise through 90°.

Further Work

Setting the map with the compass is one of the main uses of a compass in orienteering. Encourage pupils to do this with every map they use.

Use map orientation and bearing exercises for further practice (p76,77).

MAP SETTING AND BEARING EXERCISES

AIM
- *to practise following a good line with an orientated map or compass bearing in a very familiar area*

EQUIPMENT CHECKLIST

Map orientation (setting) can be attempted with a map guide compass, a thumb compass or a protractor compass. This exercise can be used to introduce the thumb compass and running with the map and compass together. Note that compass bearings can only be practised with a protractor compass.

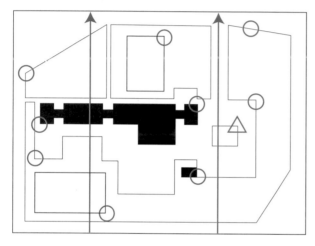

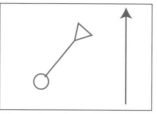

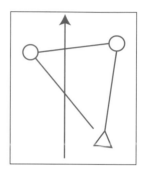

Examples of course cards

Preparation

Check that the map to be used has magnetic north lines. Select 8 - 12 control sites on easy distinctive features. Avoid putting controls out too close together, or legs through buildings. Controls should be no more than 150m from base. Each control should have a code letter. Procedure is like a star exercise (p27).

Prepare course cards (see illustration) - traced off the main master map. Cards could have one, two or more points to visit. Use a pin point to get the centre of each circle accurate. Include descriptions on a course card if controls are out of sight of the start. The map sections can be cut small, fixed to stiff card and covered if they are to be used again.

Use the master to put out small control markers (micro markers taped to pegs are easy to use).

Practical

Demonstrate the importance of first lining up the needle with the magnetic north lines carefully, then looking ahead along the line of travel before moving off. Always stand at the start point facing the direction you want to go.

Give out cards. Visit controls and remember the code letters.

Adaptation

Such courses can be set up in a park or wooded area. Legs should not be longer then 150m. Complete courses with 4-6 controls can be planned on a blank map for practising compass skills and distance judgement. The distance can be given, e.g. start - 1 = 60m. If the map is to scale the distance can be measured. Several courses can be planned to avoid following.

Compass skills are practised in many of the technique training exercises. The best ones for beginners are 'traffic light orienteering' (p58) and 'rough orienteering' (p79).

Further work

Once pupils have mastered the use of the compass for setting their map, it is possible to progress and develop the technique of using both map and protractor compass together in the same hand.

This technique is widely used by orienteers to keep the map set at all times. It is good to develop this skill early on with beginners.

Place the compass on the map with the edge along the line of travel (or a little to one side to avoid obscuring detail). Hold the compass and map together in one hand. The map needs to be folded small.

Turn the map and yourself round until the floating magnetic needle points the same way as the magnetic north arrows on the map.

Now just go in the direction that the direction of travel arrow on the compass shows.

Rough orienteering and aiming off (p79).

Attack points (p87).

Self perpetuating course (p66).

Traffic light orienteering (p58).

MOVING WITH MAP AND COMPASS

AIM
• to establish the advantages of using a compass to set the map and confirm the direction of travel

EQUIPMENT CHECKLIST

Preparation

Plan two or three short courses (400-800m). Each course should follow line features only with a control at each turning point. Start and Finish should be at the same point (a very distinctive path junction). Draw two or three course master maps for students to copy, or premark one map clearly with all courses.

Tapes can be used instead of markers and as controls are on line features students could put them out as a warm up.

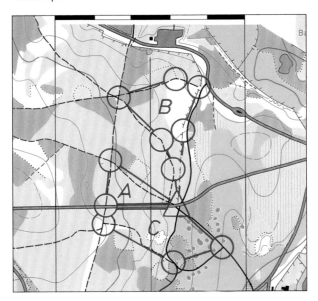

Lesson

Emphasise folding and thumbing the map, and revise setting/orientating with the compass. Note that rotating the housing of a protractor compass is not necessary. If map guide compasses are to be used, they should be clipped on to the map and checked.

COURSE A - using the needle to orientate the map

At the start and each control:

• hold the map looking forwards to the next control circle on the map.

  (Thumb compass - put the corner of the leading edge where you are. Protractor compass - put the compass edge along the path you want to follow.)

• Turn with the map until needle north points to map north (don't use the dial on a protractor compass).

• Off you go.

COURSES B & C (Thumb or Map Guide compasses)

As for course A, sorting out any difficulties before setting off.

COURSES B & C (Protractor compass)

• Take a bearing at each control.

• Hold the map looking forward to the next control.

• Put the compass edge along the line feature you want to follow.

• Turn (dial) the compass housing until north-south lines of the housing are parallel with those of the map.

• Turn so that needle north, compass north and map north are all the same way.

• The direction of travel arrow should point along the line feature you want to follow.

• NB The compass can be held with the map in one hand or taken off the map and held in the other hand.

Compass and map set and ready to go.

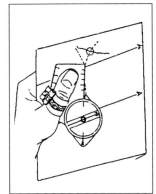
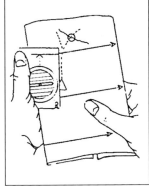

Adaptations

All courses can be planned of equal length so that students can start on A, B or C. If it is possible to progress either way round, six could start at once.

Further work

'Safety bearings' (p78) then 'rough orienteering and aiming off' (p79).

Refer to 'using the compass' (p74). Plan short exercises which demonstrate, practise and test the different uses of the compass.

SAFETY BEARINGS

AIM

• to show how the compass can be easily and usefully used to follow a cardinal direction selected from the map

EQUIPMENT CHECKLIST

A safety bearing is a direction which, if followed, will bring the orienteer to a major linear feature (a track or road) which leads back to the start or base. It is usually one of the 4 cardinal directions North, South, East or West.

This exercise is a good introduction to the idea of following a set direction using the compass needle only or 'dialling' the direction with a protractor compass. It also reinforces the fact that if you know where North is you can work out any other direction.

These exercises can be used as a progressive series or selected according to circumstances.

Preparation

Plan a series of exercises using the ideas presented below. Make a collection of maps containing clear boundaries, plot a course or several control points to use for reference.

Map guide, thumb compasses or protractor compasses can be used.

Practical

Look at the maps and discuss

. . . which roads or tracks would be best to head for if you wanted to get back to the finish or 'base',

. . . which of the cardinal directions you would follow.

With a protractor compass practise dialling and facing each direction.

N
W ← → **E**
S

CLASSROOM OR HALL OR PLAYGROUND

Practise facing then moving towards each direction by looking at the magnetic needle.

a) without a plan

b) with a plan

In the playground head for definite features.

HALL, PLAYGROUND OR WOODLAND

Walk a square.

Leave an object, e.g., a glove or stick, at the start.

Walk the same distance in each direction, e.g. 5 paces.

Return as close as possible to the start point.

Using the compass with a map or plan is more realistic.

Repeat with smaller object, e.g. a coin, or a different number of paces.

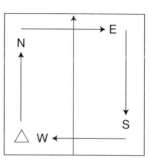

WOODLAND

Take a group into an area of woodland with distinct boundaries. Give out a map and compass each.

Discuss the best safety direction to refind base (bus?).

Check each person is holding the map and compass correctly before allowing them to go.

e.g. North to road, follow it eastwards.

Return to base.

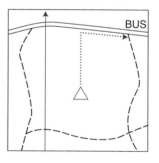

Put out controls on each junction round the area of woodland. Lead group into the middle of the area.

The teacher selects a control, pupils select the safety direction, e.g. for control D, safety direction is south or west.

All meet at D.

Repeat in the same or a different area with pupils working in pairs. A leads partner into the area. B selects a control. Together or separately they decide on the safety direction and go to the control.

e.g. north or east to find B.

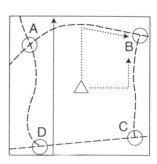

ROUGH ORIENTEERING AND AIMING OFF

AIM
• to increase confidence in using a compass for cutting corners and 'rough' orienteering

EQUIPMENT CHECKLIST

Rough orienteering using a compass is taking an accurate bearing but running fast on it, knowing that there are collecting features to keep you in contact with the map.

With a thumb compass, the leading edge is placed beside the direction of travel and the needle and map north kept together when running. Much attention is paid to picking up major features from the map.

A protractor compass can be held in two ways; with the map in one hand and the edge of the compass along the direction of travel, running with the needle set to map north; or it can be held in the opposite hand with an accurate bearing taken from the map.

Fine orienteering involves taking much more care about direction, distance and reading detail.

Preparation

Use an area with a network of tracks, paths, rides etc. Put controls on line feature junctions so that the course cuts diagonally across the blocks of woodland (see example). Plan 3 loops or a course divided into 2 or 3 sections or a course that can be repeated. Keep each loop/section under 2 kilometres.

Practical

Teach and practise one point at a time when first introducing these skills.

The group puts out controls as a warm up (see map).

Start - 4: take a bearing straight to each control. Run, trying to stay on the bearing; look ahead as far as possible and glance at the compass every 30-50 metres (4-8 seconds) to recheck the needle is still aligned correctly. If you hit a line feature and it is not obvious which way to turn, orientate the map with the compass to establish which line feature you are on.

4 - 7: aim off by taking the bearing about 50m to one side of the control (edge of the circle). Start slowly and increase speed once you are confident of hitting the feature on the side of the control that you are aiming for.

Alternatively aim off by taking a bearing to the control but running with a left or right inclination. Deliberately keep to one side of the bearing. Decide which method of aiming off you prefer.

Test over a timed course which could be slightly longer.

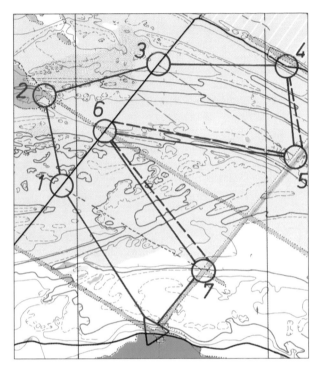

Course divided into two sections

S-4 a bearing straight to each control,

4-7 aiming off.

Adaptations

1 This exercise could usefully be done in pairs, the one behind trying to keep in contact with the map. Change over after 3-4 controls, not alternate ones, to allow rhythm to develop.

2 Include pacing practice with running on a bearing. It builds confidence because you can't miss the controls!

Further work

Blank map exercises (p76), compass and pacing exercises (p82), exercises on attack points (p42) and traffic lights (p58). Encourage the use of rough and fine compass work.

FINE ORIENTEERING - CONTROL PICKING

AIM
• *to improve accurate use of the compass with pacing and map contact*

EQUIPMENT CHECKLIST

Fine orienteering is used when you must know precisely where you are. It is necessary most often on courses where controls are away from line features. Accurate navigation is used to find the control feature from an attack point. Map contact needs to be maintained with the help of a mental picture. Distance estimation should be precise and the compass followed slowly and carefully.

The most useful (and traditional) exercises for fine orienteering are line orienteering and control picking. Line orienteering tests map contact while control picking gives the opportunity to use accurate compass bearings with pacing as well as map contact.

Lesson

No timing. Explain the purpose of the exercise.

• to follow compass direction very carefully

• to measure distance and pace count

• to create a mental picture of the ground

Allow a minimum of two minutes between starts to prevent individuals gaining advantage from seeing others ahead.

Discuss the exercise afterwards. Did they use the compass and pace count? Did it work?

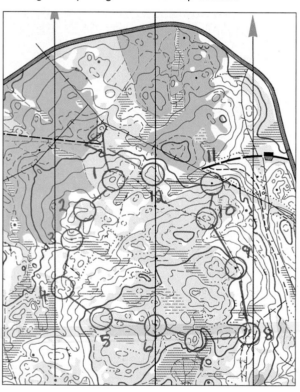

Control descriptions:

1 Knoll

2 Knoll, East end

3 Earth wall

4 Re-entrant

5 Spur, top

6 Small knoll

7 Knoll

8 Crag foot

9 Boulder

10 Knoll

Preparation - control picking

Select an area with plenty of detail, good catching features and an accurate map. Plan a short course (1.5 - 3 km) where each control is the attack point for the next. Control sites should be small (boulder, knoll, depression, etc.) to encourage precise compass work and pacing. Leg lengths should be under 300m, 100-200m being most realistic. Mini controls may be used with an experienced group. Hang controls low but do not hide them.

Further work

Traffic lights (p58).

Corridor orienteering (p55).

See the Training & Coaching manual for more work on fine orienteering.

TAKING A BEARING ON THE MOVE

AIMS
- *to encourago taking compass bearings on the move*
- *to introduce the compass into control flow*

EQUIPMENT CHECKLIST

Preparation

Whatever the experience of the group, plan a very simple course of 0.5-1.5 km. The course should involve plenty of changes of direction. Controls should be on paths to enable easy movement whilst handling the map and compass.

Hang out the controls (with punches) visible from 20-50 metres away.

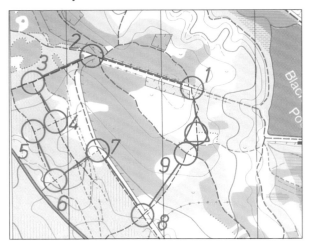

Lesson

Practise taking compass bearings from the map, first standing, then walking.

Explain the procedure for the exercise below and demonstrate. Remind everyone about folding and thumbing their maps.

- From the start run towards the first control.

- Once the control is visible, but before reaching it, take a bearing from the first control along the path to second control. Walk if necessary but DO NOT STOP.

- Punch the card at the first control.

- Move off in the right direction, checking the compass.

- As soon as the second control is visible take a bearing from the control along the track towards the third control

Try to maintain this rhythm concentrating on taking a bearing **on the move** and **before you reach the control**. If possible go out to one of the first three controls to watch or help individuals as necessary. Once this routine is established it can be practised on a normal course or at an event.

CONTROL FLOW

Control flow is the rhythm of orienteering through controls with minimum time wasted in slowing down or stopping to read the map and make decisions. It is developed by having a **system** of planning one leg ahead and moving quickly through controls.

Courses with easy legs or easy parts to each leg are best for introducing a **system**. Traffic light orienteering (p58) can be used, where the next leg is planned in the 'green' phase.

Further work

A playground exercise to practise. Prepare by collecting maps - from competitions, other orienteers.

Everyone should have a map and a control card.

Mark out two circles with one control marker and plenty of punches right in the centre. The outer circle should be large enough for all the group to run round without tripping each other up.

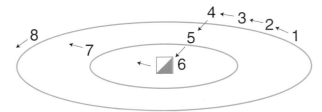

1 Run round the outside of the outer ring with the map, select an attack point to the first control.

2 Take a bearing or set the thumb compass as if you are at the attack point, about to go into the control.

3 When you reach the point on the circle when the compass points to the control, follow it in towards the marker.

*4 **Before you cross** the **inner** circle take a bearing or reset the thumb compass for the direction you want to **leave** the control depending on your route choice.*

5 Punch your card at the marker and move away to the outer circle following the compass.

6 Continue round the outer circle and select the attack point to the second control. Repeat steps 3-6.

7 Repeat this routine until the course is finished.

Practise on a course or at the next competition.

COMPASS AND PACING

AIM
• to practise or test the protractor compass and pacing skills in terrain

EQUIPMENT CHECKLIST
card, base peg

Preparation

Select an area with good visibility. Mark out a number of (coloured) taped routes from a central point.

Take bearings and measure distance from the end of each taped route to 3 features 50-200 metres away. Use a feature on the map for the end of each taped route otherwise it will be necessary to use a sighting compass or someone else to check that bearings are accurate.

Hang controls and punches on the selected features.

Write down the bearing and distance for each feature on a card. Include the feature description to encourage observation of the terrain.

Set out the cards at the end of each taped route so that they cannot blow away.

Make up instruction sheets for ease of explanation.

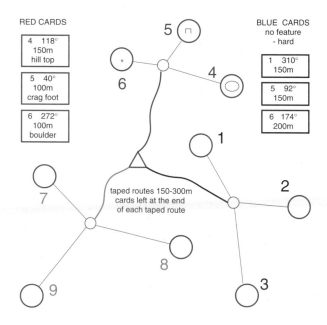

RED CARDS

| 4 118° |
| 150m |
| hill top |

| 5 40° |
| 100m |
| crag foot |

| 6 272° |
| 100m |
| boulder |

BLUE CARDS
no feature
- hard

| 1 310° |
| 150m |

| 5 92° |
| 150m |

| 6 174° |
| 200m |

taped routes 150-300m
cards left at the end
of each taped route

Practical

Explain the exercise. The only equipment needed is a protractor compass.

Divide the class into the same number of groups as taped routes. Each person in the group completes the three legs before moving on to the next three.

Finish when all controls have been visited and punched.

Further work

Introductory exercises on pacing can be found on p45. Those familiar with compass bearings and pacing can practise in school grounds with the following exercise.

Give each person two blank pieces of paper or card, something to hold the card down on the ground such as a peg or stone, and a code letter (if required).

Allocate a number to each member of the group.

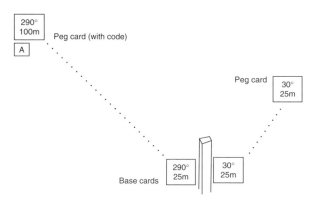

| 290° |
| 100m |

| A |

Peg card (with code)

Peg card

| 30° |
| 25m |

| 290° |
| 25m |

| 30° |
| 25m |

Base cards

Everyone chooses a bearing and distance and writes them on both pieces of paper. Keep distances under 150m (less if the area available is limited). To avoid duplication of bearings offer each pupil a limited range to select from - 1 to 50, 51 to 100, 101 to 150. Their number should be written on the back of the card.

Establish a base and put a peg in the ground. Each pupil then puts out one of their cards (and code letter) at the right bearing and distance from the base peg.

The group keeps exchanging cards, finding as many locations as possible in a limited time. Start by standing directly in front of the base peg each time. Discrepancies should be checked by the teacher.

With relative beginners make the cards very visible.

Other exercises to use:

Window orienteering (p56). Rough orienteering and aiming off (p79). Compass bearing exercise in school field (p76). Game - bearing and distance (p103).

Exercises such as attack points (p42), traffic light orienteering (p58) and self perpetuating courses (p66) can be planned to encourage the use of pacing with compass.

7

THEORY SESSIONS

These sessions can be used as short 15-30 minute classroom exercises which are aids to practical orienteering. It is important to recognise that the theory sessions are not an end in themselves but a platform for **practice**. Most teaching takes place when students are actively involved in the skills and techniques of the orienteering. The theoretical concepts explain **why** the practical ensures the **how**.

MAP SYMBOLS AND SCALE

AIMS
- *to teach basic symbols and colours*
- *to teach scale*

EQUIPMENT CHECKLIST
map legends +

Lesson

There are internationally agreed symbols, colours and scales for orienteering maps.

MAP SYMBOLS

The colours used for orienteering maps are different from conventional maps and reflect orienteering's origin as a forest sport (full list of symbols on p141).

Some symbols use two colours but in general terms colours are used as follows:

Black	Man made features, rock, danger
Blue	Water features
Brown	Land form features
Yellow	Open land (no trees)
Green	Dense forest and undergrowth
White	Woodland without dense vegetation

Go through all the map symbols by colours. As an aid to learning, symbols of each colour could be made into a wall poster. Give out maps with a clear legend. Students select a colour and create a poster.

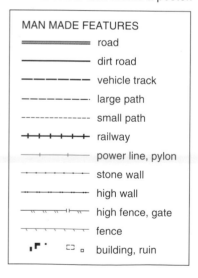

STRESS
- that woodland is represented by white and green
- that yellow shows open ground with good visibility
- that magnetic north lines are used

Follow this up with symbol recognition games, card games (p95), orienteering bingo (p98), drawing maps (p99) and worksheet (p106).

SCALE

Orienteering maps use various scales.

1:15,000 is used for competition maps.
1:10,000 is used for competition and training maps.
1:5,000 is commonly used for local parks.
1:2,500 is suitable for school grounds.

Although scale is expressed as a ratio - 1:10,000 means one unit on the map represents 10,000 units on the ground - the easiest way to teach scale is to get pupils to measure 100m on the map using the scale bar. The correct scale bar to be used will depend on the map.

SCALE BARS

1:15,000	0m 100 200 300 400 500 600 700 800 900
1:10,000	0m 100 200 300 400 500 600
1:5,000	0m 50 100 200 300
1:2,500	0 metres 50 100 150

Cut out a scale bar from an old map or copy one of those above. Tape it to one edge of the compass or paste it on to a longer piece of card.

Pupils should familiarise themselves with what a distance of 100m looks like on the ground and on the map. The scale bars above are easier to understand than actually measuring distances in millimetres on the map and converting to metres on the ground.

At 1:10,000
1mm on the map = 10,000mm (10m) on the ground
10mm on the map = 100m on the ground

At 1: 15,000
1mm on map = 15,000mm (15m) on ground
10mm on the map = 150m on the ground
(6.67mm on the map = 100m on the ground)

The concept of scale is introduced in 'understanding maps' (p19), distance measurement (p102).

Further work

Distance estimation (p44), pacing (p45), games and worksheets (chapter 8)

These topics can also lead on to work in mathematics and geography.

SETTING AND THUMBING THE MAP

AGE GROUP
TIME   10-30min

AIMS
• to help pupils appreciate the importance of keeping their map set
• to demonstrate the importance of keeping their position pinpointed with the thumb on the map

EQUIPMENT CHECKLIST

Lesson

SETTING THE MAP

It is much easier to navigate if the map is orientated to the ground - directions on the map will be the same as on the ground. To demonstrate this:

Draw a plan of the classroom or just the positions of people round a table. Set it correctly and ask who is sitting where on the plan. Now set it incorrectly and ask again who is where. It will be clear that it is much more difficult with the map set incorrectly.

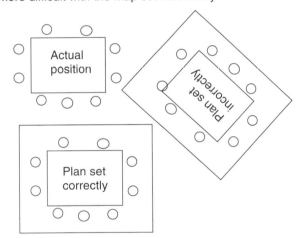

NOTE: there are two methods of setting a map

1 Using features on the ground:

turn the map until the line features on it are lying in the same direction as the same features on the ground.

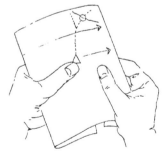

2 Using a compass:

turn the map until the magnetic north lines are parallel to and going the same way as the magnetic north needle in the compass.

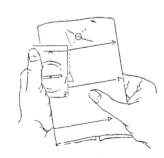

THUMBING THE MAP

Prepare plans of the classroom and set out a course with legs in a north, south, east and west direction whenever possible. Use 5-8 controls. Mark the north side of the map clearly with a red line.

Discuss direction from the map, knowing that the top of the map is north, e.g. go north to control 1, west to control 2. Then proceed as follows.

1 Identify north in the room and stick up a large N.

2 Hold the map with the thumb on the start looking towards control 1. Fold the map if necessary.

3 Turn until the north end of the map (the red end) is to the north in the room. Follow the direction from the thumb towards control 1.

4 At control 1, put your thumb on control 1 looking towards control 2.

5 Turn so that map north is to room north.

6 Continue round the course establishing the same procedure on each leg.

Concentrate on holding the map correctly with the thumb on the control and turning so the map north is to room north. Don't distract them with a lot of discussion on what features are being followed - this can be done during a later lesson on map legend and simple route choice.

Introduce the compass needle. Establish N, S, E, W looking at the magnetic needle only (it should be the same as room north). Repeat stages 3-6 looking at the compass needle to set the map rather than features in the room. Initially don't worry if the compass is held incorrectly. Remember that metal objects may affect a magnetic compass needle!

In future lessons the same procedure and course can be used for putting the compass on the map along the line of each leg, or using the same course for taking and following a bearing with a protractor compass.

Further work

The first classroom lessons (chapter 2) are also useful for teaching map orientation.

Using the compass to set the map (p72).

LINE FEATURES AS HANDRAILS

AIM

• *to demonstrate how line features can be used to select safe and fast route choices*

EQUIPMENT CHECKLIST

Once pupils understand the basic meaning of the map they need to learn how to use it. When trying to navigate from one point to another it is best to form a plan of action. Line features used as part of this plan are called 'handrails'. They offer safe and fast routes.

Lesson

When you start an orienteering course you need to plan how to get from one point to the next. At the start set your map and make sure you know which features on the map represent the features on the ground.

Then work out a plan of action for getting to the first control. The first things to look for on the map are line features such as roads, paths, walls, fences at the edge of fields, ditches or even distinct vegetation changes. These are easy to follow and will lead you along your route. If you keep the map set at all times you will know which way to turn to follow the lines. Work in this way control by control. The question is 'what do I follow?'

Some examples are illustrated opposite.

Using lines in a roundabout way is safer than trying to shortcut corners.

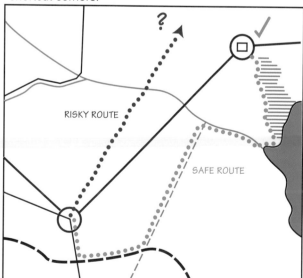

Give each child an orienteering map with a course marked on it that has simple line feature route choices. They write down the line features they would follow between each control.

See also route choice in worksheet 2 (p107).

EXAMPLES

a) A very straightforward course with all controls linked by two line features used as 'handrails'

4-5: follow the edge of the field (yellow) then the edge of the thicker trees (green) to the control.

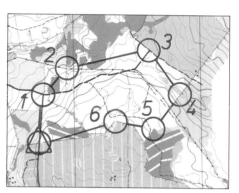

b) A choice of paths to follow - not always as easy as it looks.

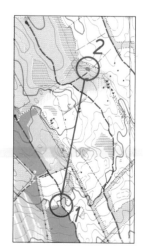

c) Which routes would you take? How many different line features would you use for 'handrails'?

ATTACK POINTS

AIM
* to establish the idea of selecting an attack point when planning routes
  between controls

EQUIPMENT CHECKLIST

An attack point is an obvious and precise feature close to the control from which the control can be located, for example using a bearing and accurate distance judgement.

Lesson

When controls are on point features such as marshes or boulders, or on contour features such as knolls or spurs, you have to leave the line features to find them.

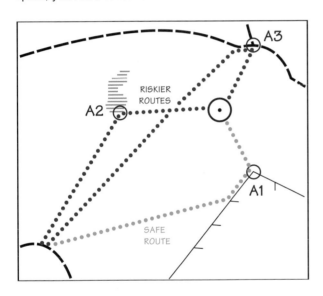

Blackboard diagram

Remember that there may be several possible attack points ranging in difficulty and 'safety' for finding a control. Beginners should choose a safe route to a large, obvious attack point even if the distance is greater.

A1   safe route - longer

A2   risky - may miss attack point and then may miss the control

A3   middle route - may miss the control

Further work

Practical (p42)

Traffic lights orienteering (p58)

ATTACK POINT THEORY

a) The fence corner is the nearest definite point before the control - this is the ATTACK POINT.

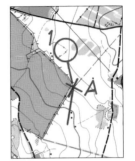

b) The junction of the bank, path and ride is the obvious ATTACK POINT for this leg. The route choice is to the attack point, not straight to the control.

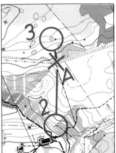

c) The wall corner and road/path junction offer a choice of two ATTACK POINTS which will influence the route choice.

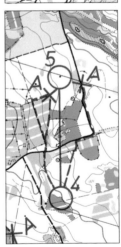

d) The ATTACK POINT here is the steeper part of the major re-entrant.

e) If there is a choice of 'attacking' a control from above or below, it is better to go in from above - giving you more visibility.

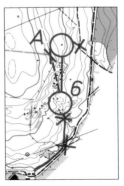

COLLECTING FEATURES

AIM
• *to demonstrate the use of collecting features*

EQUIPMENT CHECKLIST

A collecting feature is an obvious feature beyond the control which you will hit if you miss the control from your attack point. A collecting feature may also be used to check location en route to the attack point.

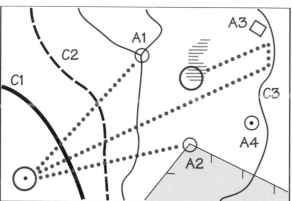

Blackboard diagram

Lesson

Each large feature you come across on your way to an attack point is an 'en route' collecting feature and should be checked off on your map.

An obvious large or linear feature beyond the control will act as a 'safety' collecting feature if the control is overshot or missed. If this happens return to your attack point or use a secondary attack point.

Tick off collecting features (C1, C2) as you cross them until you get to your attack point A1 or A2. The stream beyond the control is a 'safety' collecting feature (C3) and the two secondary attack points are the ruin (A3) and boulder (A4).

Give each child a map. Ask each child to make up legs demonstrating collecting features behind the controls and identifying large collecting features between control sites.

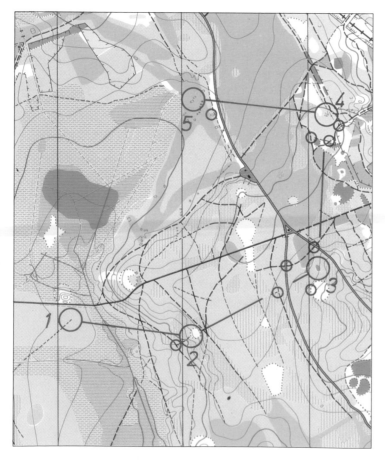

EXAMPLES

All these legs have plenty of collecting features 'en route' and behind as 'safety' if the control is missed.

1-2   The stream and tracks make good collecting features if you go straight.

2-3   The road is the major collecting feature but checking off the paths before the road gives you confidence that you are going the right way.

The road behind the control is a collecting feature if you miss the thicket.

3-4   The track and the edge of the wood-land are collecting features and also <u>handrails</u> leading to an <u>attack point</u>.

4-5   The road and the path before the control are good collecting features but it is important to know <u>exactly</u> where you are before leaving the path as the knolls may not be obvious.

AIMING OFF

AIM
• to demonstrate the most effective way to find a precise point on a long line feature

EQUIPMENT CHECKLIST

Lesson

When heading for a point or control on a long feature, the most effective way of finding it is to deliberately aim to one side so that when you reach the feature and cannot see the control you know which way to turn to find it. This technique is called AIMING OFF.

Aiming off can be used in several situations. In this case the stream junction is the attack point - you aim off either side of this. To find the control aim off to the right of it - then you will definitely hit the marsh.

NB Competent orienteers usually aim only slightly off the control site leaving less distance to run when the turn is made.

Advantages of aiming off:

1   You can move faster because you are running for a long feature rather than a precise point.

2   You can run more confidently as you are certain of hitting the long feature and can then run directly to the control.

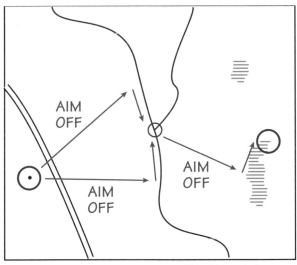

Blackboard diagram

Practical

Rough orienteering and aiming off (p79).

EXAMPLES

A B C

To find controls on line features - deliberately aim to one side of the control to be sure of turning the right way and finding the control first time.

D E F

To find controls close to line features - aim to one side of the control, then travel parallel to the line feature at the correct distance from it, e.g. to find E - aim above the control, pace 50m beyond the stream, then turn down hill (south) until you see the control.

G H

'Making the control longer' - the knoll and cliff are at the end of two distinctive spurs. By aiming off to the spur above you are led into the control by following the spur.

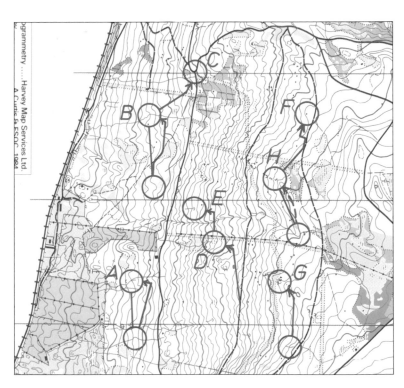

INTRODUCTION TO CONTOURS

AIMS
• to introduce the concept of contours
• to develop visual interpretation of the shape and steepness of the ground

EQUIPMENT CHECKLIST
sand tray, orange wool

A contour joins points of equal height on the ground and is shown by a brown line on the map. The main job of the contours is to indicate the shape and steepness of the ground.
- the closer the lines, the steeper the slope.
- if there are no lines, the ground is flat.
- hill tops are shown by ring contours.
- re-entrants bend in towards the top of the hill.
- spurs bend out like a 'nose' away from the hill, etc.

On orienteering maps the contour interval (the vertical height between contours) is usually 5 metres.

Practical exercises

1 Give everyone a contour only map with plenty of features on it, and 2-3 coloured pencils or highlighters.

• Mark all the hill tops with one colour. How many?
• Find one contour line, as long as possible - colour it. What shapes are made?
• Look for valleys and re-entrants. Draw a line along the valley bottom - new colour.
• Colour in the spurs.

2 Use trays filled with sand.

• Demonstrate making shapes using the sand with orange wool or twine as contour lines.
- a single hill, 3 contours high. Look from above.
- a hill with re-entrants, spurs, steep and flat ground.

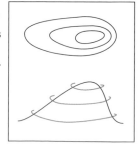

• In small groups - make hills and contour features
- similar to the demonstration model
- to match a contour map.

3 Contour 'Donkey'

• Draw a large contour map with all the basic shapes on it. Copy to use by groups of 4.

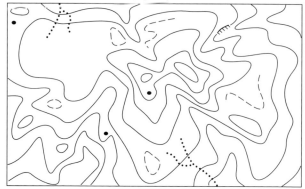

• Make labels: | Hill top | Knoll | Re-entrant | Spur |
| Steep ground | Flat ground | Pit | Saddle | Gully |

• Put the maps up round the room, one for each group. Work in pairs. One is blindfolded with a label and pin or adhesive tape then directed verbally by the other to fix the label on the correct point of the map.

NOTE

Form lines are dashed brown lines which improve the picture of the ground for the orienteer. They are extra lines which would not be shown by the regular contour interval.

Tags are sometimes shown on the downhill side of the contour to clarify which is the downhill direction.

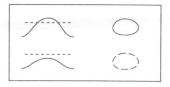

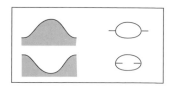

4 Mark the building you are in with 5 metre flags or tape.

5 Quiz using maps with contour features. Include questions from Worksheet 2 (p107).

CONTOUR MODELS

AGE GROUP	11+
TIME	5-30min

AIM
• *to improve pupils' ability to understand contours*

EQUIPMENT CHECKLIST
polystyrene tiles, glue

Preparation

Prepare a simple contour map as shown below.

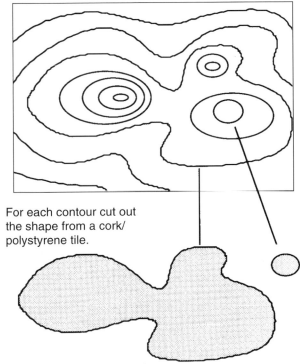

For each contour cut out the shape from a cork/polystyrene tile.

Stick the shapes on top of each other to form a model.

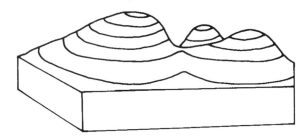

The model can be 'smoothed' as shown in the diagram to make it more realistic or it can be 'stepped', the edges of the tiles left square forming ledges.

Practical

Use the models and corresponding map diagrams to demonstrate the function of contours (see opposite).

Produce a variety of models showing different contour features, or one model with a variety of features on it.

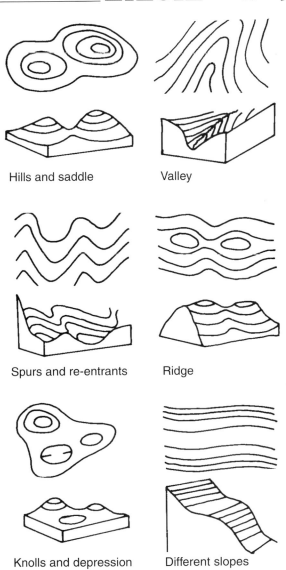

Hills and saddle

Valley

Spurs and re-entrants

Ridge

Knolls and depression

Different slopes

Adaptations and further work

Pupils can make their own contour models.

Make contour models from real maps.

More experienced pupils can use the models to help the less experienced.

Refer to Coaching Videos 1 and 2.
A variety of teaching aids - sand trays, potato cuts, stones in water - are used in contour understanding.

Introduction to contours (p49), contour perception (p69).

8

INDOOR GAMES AND EXERCISES

MAN THE MASTER MAPS

AGE GROUP	5-12
TIME	10 min

AIMS
* *to reinforce the cardinal compass directions and other orienteering terms*
* *to warm up a group before more serious orienteering or physical activity*

EQUIPMENT CHECKLIST
N (north) card

A warm-up fun game to get rid of excess energy. It runs in a similar way to the school game 'Shipwrecks'.

Preparation

No preparation apart from making a large N to go at the north end of the room.

Practical

The leader calls

"Go North"

> Everyone runs to the North end of the room/hall.

"Go South, West, East ..."

"Man the master maps"

> On to hands and knees - bottoms in the air!

"Lost? Don't panic"

> Hug the person nearest to you.

"Relocation"

> Turning 360° with hand to forehead looking for some recognisable feature.

"Trip over a log"

> Something resembling a rugby tackle without an opponent.

"Stuck in a bog"

> Lie on one side with one arm and leg in the air.

"Sprint to the finish"

> Racing into a space or running on the spot.

Introduce one or two calls at a time to establish reactions.

Variations

Last one to perform on each call is out - last one left at the end is the winner.

A child does the calling.

JIGSAWS

AGE GROUP	9+
TIME	5-30 min

AIM
• *to encourage pupils to look at maps*

EQUIPMENT CHECKLIST
card, glue, clear self-adhesive film

Preparation and practical

These are very simple to prepare and can be made to varying degrees of difficulty. It is advisable to paste the map on to card or board, and cover with clear plastic self-adhesive film. Edges cut with pinking shears help to keep the map pieces together.

The example below shows various ways of cutting the pieces to make it more or less difficult.

A   Different curvy shapes - easy

B   Straighter shapes - more difficult

C   Symmetrical shapes - very difficult

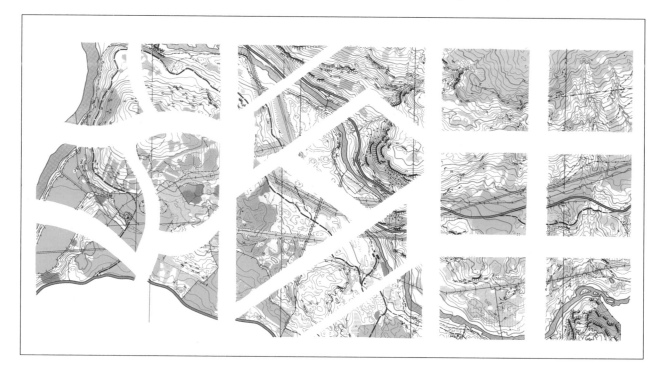

Adaptations and further work

(These are made easier if a pupil has a master copy to look at.)

Contour-only jigsaw maps - very difficult.

Maps cut into smaller pieces.

Running game: *jigsaw pieces are put at one end of the hall. Children run with one piece at a time to the other end and make up the jigsaw. A whole map to look at helps beginners.*

Group mixing game: *get several copies of the same map, and cut each map into 3 pieces in different ways. Give out a piece of map to each member of the group i.e. 12 people would have 4 cut up maps. Try to split people from same class, club, school, etc. Each person then has to go round and find the other two pieces (people) to make a complete map. The result will be groups of 3. Follow up with a group exercise or team game e.g. team score (p43) or point to point relay.*

Picture maps and playground maps: *put a map onto plywood and cut into pieces such that major features are on different pieces. In groups or as individuals identify features and put in correct position. A frame is useful to hold the jigsaw together. See picture maps (p25,142).*

CARD GAMES

AIM

• to improve pupils' familiarity with maps and symbols

EQUIPMENT CHECKLIST
prepared cards

Preparation

Several card sets can be easily made and used in various ways. Sets are best made in pairs - one half of the set being numbered (say 1-20), the other half being lettered (A-T). Cards can be paired according to physical or technical difficulty. Keep a sheet showing correct pair answers. Use different coloured card for each half of a set to ease identification.

There are variations on the main theme of pairing the cards in the sets. Pairs are made as follows:

SET A: symbol + name. Several sets of these can be used to help a class learn the basic map symbols - black set, blue set, brown set, etc. Large hand drawn sets can be made instead of cutting up map legends. Alternatively include both with written names to make sets of 3.

SET B: same pieces of map in each pair.

SET C: same pieces of map but orientated differently on card. Controls could also be drawn on different control sites to make it harder.

SET D: full colour map section + same map without black (if available).

SET E: full colour map + contour-only map of the same section.

SET F: map section + photograph.

Practical

Methods of pairing:

1 Simply match cards while sitting at a table.

2 Write down matching card number and letter, e.g. 2 and C for set A. This way several pupils can use the same map set.

3 In a hall, put half of each set at one end and half at the other. In teams they have to run to one end, memorise a card and return to find the correct pair. One set per team.

4 Write down one number, run to the other end, work out its pair and write down the letter next to the number. Some brighter pupils may be able to carry more than one card in their memory.

5 Snap - for this you need several copies of the set.

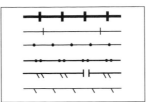

railway	
power line, pylon	
stone wall	
high wall	
high fence, gate	
fence	

SET A   Symbols + names

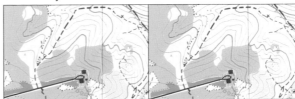

SET B   Pieces of map (same)

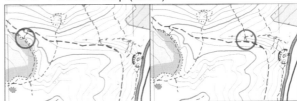

SET C   Same map with different controls

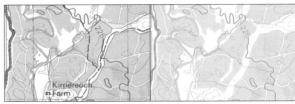

SET D   Same map - one with no black

SET E   Map + contour-only map

SET F   Map + photograph

Adaptations and further work

See physical and mental fitness (p116).

FILL IN THE BLANKS

AIM
* *to encourage pupils to look at maps in detail and recognise patterns*

EQUIPMENT CHECKLIST
card, glue, clear self-adhesive film

Preparation

Puzzles can be easily prepared by cutting up old maps and protecting the pieces with a transparent self-adhesive film.

Several different types of puzzles can be made of varying degrees of difficulty.

Examples shown opposite:

A1 (top): one complete map with boxes drawn on showing where pieces fit. Pieces are cut out of another map of the same area.

A2 (middle): one complete map with no boxes drawn on. Pieces are cut out of another map of the same area.

A3 (bottom): one map with holes from which the pieces have been cut. Pieces have to be fitted into the holes. This is a more difficult variation.

Practical

Matching the pieces to the map can be done round a table or it can be turned into a running game (see previous page).

Adaptations and further work

To make the puzzles easier, different sizes and shapes can be cut out. It becomes more of a shape-matching exercise but it does lead students to look at the map.

To make the exercise more difficult the pieces can be stuck on to cards and numbered, likewise with the holes (lettered) - see A3. Pupils have to match the map patterns in their head and note the numbers/letters rather than by physically piecing them together.

Puzzles can be used in a running game. Look at a piece at one end of the hall, run to the other end and there mark the outline on the blank map with a pencil. Alternatively take the piece and place it on the correct section of the map.

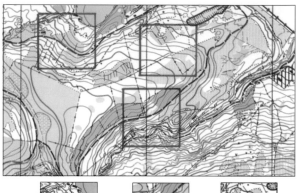

A1 Map with boxes drawn to show where pieces fit.

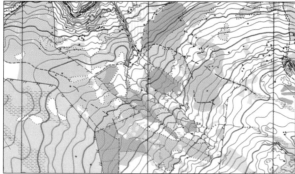

A2 Map without boxes drawn.

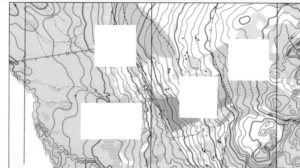

A3 Map pieces cut out a more difficult variation.

MEMORY GAMES

AIM
• *to help pupils to practise map and course memory and recall*

EQUIPMENT CHECKLIST

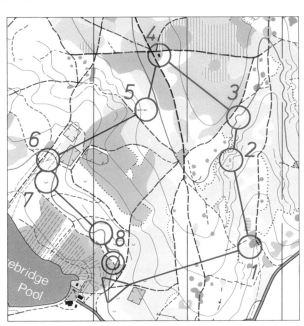

Memory games are those where one feature, part of a map or even a whole course has to be committed to memory for a short length of time. They are a good way of testing skills from basic line feature recognition to selection of an attack point, or remembering and redrawing what is in a control circle or several circles.

They are most fun when combined with running and a team situation. They can be inside, in the playground or back garden, anywhere - even up a hill!

Preparation and practical

Collect maps, paper and pencils for the game selected. Orienteering clubs often have a supply of out of date maps which can be used.

Game 1

TEAMS OF 2: first to do 10, or as many as possible in 3 minutes.

1   Look at control feature.   Write down name of feature, e.g. building.

or
2   Look at control feature.   Draw it.

3   Look at control circle.   Draw features in the circle. (Can you do 3 at once?)

Game 2

1   Look at leg . . .   What line feature to follow?

2   Look at leg . . .   Draw or describe route to next control

3   Look at leg . . .   Write down attack point

4   Look at course . . .   Draw major route choice features and control features - as many visits back to map as necessary.

Game 3

Pupils receive a map with a route drawn on.

They are given a set time to study it and then they are given a blank map of the area.

They have to draw their course on to the blank map.

The original course could also have a route drawn on - this makes the exercise more difficult.

The time lapse between seeing the course and drawing it up can vary - from 15 seconds to days.

Adaptations and further work

To provide added challenge and interest pupils could be asked to draw a map adequate enough for someone to use to get round the course. This is best done leg by leg.

The premarked map should be at one end of the hall, paper at the other end. Pupils run back to the map as many times as necessary to draw the course.

This could be made into a team game. The controls have to be visited, words or letters are collected which give a clue to the code word to find the 'treasure'. All controls must be found by using the drawing, not the map.

O BINGO

AIM
• *to help pupils to learn to recognise map symbols*

AGE GROUP   9+
TIME   15-30 min

EQUIPMENT CHECKLIST
counters, cover-up pieces

Preparation

Prepare an invented master map with about 30 different symbols on it. Some should be line features, some point features.

Prepare player maps, each having the same basic contour pattern but only showing 10 of the symbols on the master map. Each player map should show a different 10 symbols. Sharing one map between two would save preparation time. It is a good idea to have a basic contour pattern, and maybe a lake, common to all maps to make it look more realistic.

Prepare a set of counters, each showing a different map symbol. A broomstick cut into 10mm sections is ideal for this. Prepare a lot of cover-up pieces (card) for covering both line and point features on the map.

Practical

This game is played just like ordinary bingo.

One person is the caller and has the master map and a bag of counters. A counter is drawn, the name of the symbol on it is called out and that symbol on the master map is covered up.

The players have to recognise the symbols as they are called out and cover them up on their maps.

The winner is the first one to have all the symbols on their map covered, apart from the common features like the contours and the lake.

Change player maps to play again.

Adaptations

The game can be made easier by writing the symbol names on the counters.

More advanced pupils could try producing their own game.

Players could have cards with 8-10 symbols in boxes instead of on a map.

Direction arrows could be used, e.g. travelling East along a wall.

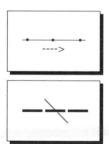

'Control sites' could also be used, e.g. track/ stream crossing.

Further work

O Bingo using other map symbols (OS, USGS, etc.):

Draw the map on a grid, one symbol on each square.

Counters show a 4-figure grid reference and a symbol.

The caller calls out the grid reference. Anyone with a symbol in that square shouts it out - correct calls get a cover up piece for that square. Alternatively the caller calls out the symbol on the counter - players search their map for the symbol and shout the grid reference.

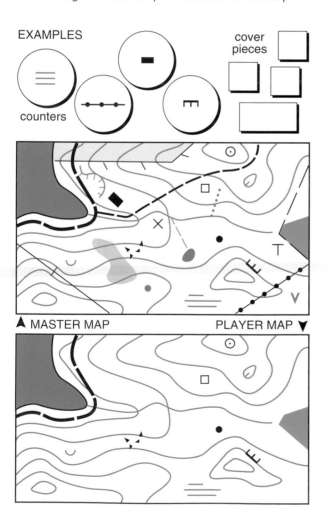

EXAMPLES   cover pieces

counters

▲ MASTER MAP   PLAYER MAP ▼

SHAKE A DICE TO DRAW A MAP

AGE GROUP	9+
TIME	15-30 min

AIM
- *to help pupils to learn map symbols*

EQUIPMENT CHECKLIST
dice, symbol list

Preparation

Make a clear list of symbols divided into six sections as shown below (about 30 symbols is an adequate number).

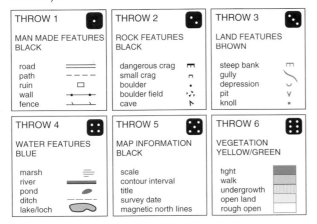

THROW 1		THROW 2		THROW 3	
MAN MADE FEATURES BLACK		**ROCK FEATURES BLACK**		**LAND FEATURES BROWN**	
road		dangerous crag		steep bank	
path		small crag		gully	
ruin		boulder		depression	
wall		boulder field		pit	
fence		cave		knoll	

THROW 4		THROW 5		THROW 6	
WATER FEATURES BLUE		**MAP INFORMATION BLACK**		**VEGETATION YELLOW/GREEN**	
marsh		scale		tight	
river		contour interval		walk	
pond		title		undergrowth	
ditch		survey date		open land	
lake/loch		magnetic north lines		rough open	

Lesson

Put the list where everyone can see it. Divide into groups with a dice and crayons. Give out a piece of paper and pencil to each pupil.

Pupils throw a dice and choose a feature out of the section with the same number as that thrown. They draw the feature on their paper and gradually make up a map with all the features. If they have all the features in one section they have to wait until the next round to throw the dice again.

The winner is the first person to have all the features drawn on their map.

More advanced pupils can draw a contour pattern on their maps first.

Adaptations

To make it more difficult the symbol list could show words only - they have to remember the symbols themselves.

Encourage pupils to draw logical and realistic maps - paths often join roads, etc.

A display of maps could be referred to at first to help beginners get started.

DRAW A MAP THEN MAKE IT

EXAMPLE OF AN INVENTED MAP

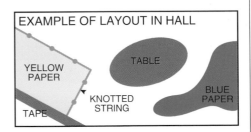

EXAMPLE OF LAYOUT IN HALL

Pupils can draw their own map.

Give them guidelines about which sort of features to put on the map (ones they can 'reconstruct' in the school hall).

A group of between 5 and 10 can use one map and use objects in the hall to reconstruct it.

This could be done outside if the weather is good.

The idea is to get them used to transferring information from map to ground and ground to map.

Sandtrays could also be used with this theme. With younger children individual shoebox 'landscapes' can be made with twigs, moss, ferns, pebbles, thread, textiles or bricks, toy animals and cars etc. Then tape a piece of clear film or cellophane over the top and use felt tip pens to draw the right shapes over the landscape. Take the 'map' off and put on a sheet of white card and compare with the landscape.

This leads on to getting pupils to draw their own maps of small areas such as gardens, houses, school halls, parkland, playground etc.

O TWISTER

AIM
• *to help pupils to learn map symbols*

EQUIPMENT CHECKLIST
dice (3), old sheet

Preparation

An ideal familiarisation exercise with a new group of 6 - 8 juniors.

Draw a map with 16 symbols - an old sheet is good for the purpose of this game. Get hold of 3 dice and an egg cup or shaker.

Write a list of the symbols in words, or words and symbols, giving each symbol a number from 3-18 (1 and 2 cannot be thrown using 3 dice).

EXAMPLE MAP

EXAMPLE LIST OF SYMBOLS
If you throw:

3	ruin	
4	boulder	
5	crag	
6	road	
7	wall	
8	large depression	
9	pit	
10	gully	
11	steep bank	
12	stream	
13	marsh	
14	pond	
15	fight	
16	open clearing	
17	knoll	
18	ditch	

Practical

Pupils take it in turns to shake the dice. Whatever the sum of the three dice is, they choose the appropriate symbol from the list.

1st throw - they put their right foot on the symbol.

2nd throw - they put their left foot on the symbol.

3rd throw - they put their right hand on the symbol.

4th throw - they put their left hand on the symbol.

5th throw - they move their right foot from its original position to put it on the new symbol.
and so on.

It is possible to have 3-4 people on the map at once.

Adaptations and further work

Instead of dice a 'spinner' could be made, possibly with 16 sides, each side having a symbol on it. A matchstick will suffice as the spindle.

The list of symbols could be just words so that they have to remember the symbol.

Pupils can work in pairs. One shakes the dice and calls the sum of the 3 dice and the appropriate feature. The other does the gymnastics described.

More symbols can be added.

Play without dice. Two teams of 2 - each has a caller and a 'do'er. Caller shouts out a symbol for the other team's 'do'er and vice versa. The winning team is the one that doesn't fall over!

COURSE PLANNING

AIMS
• to encourage pupils to look at the map in detail
• to encourage interest in course planning

AGE GROUP 11+
TIME 15-30 min

EQUIPMENT CHECKLIST

Preparation

Pupils' understanding of orienteering will benefit from some ideas about course planning. Most of this is shown in the course planning chapter (p131), but the basic ideas are described here.

Pupils are given a map to plan their course.

Practical

Plan a course bearing in mind the course planning ideas shown opposite.

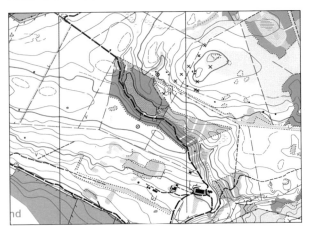

Always put controls on definite features

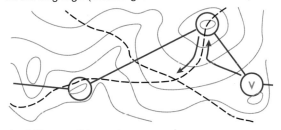

Avoid dog legs (doubling back out of a control)

Avoid impossible or dangerous legs

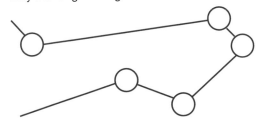

Vary the length of legs between controls

Don't make it too easy (1-3) or too difficult (3-5)

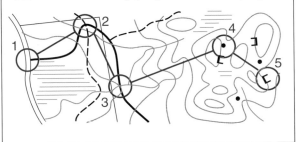

Adaptations and further work

Pupils could draw their own map and plan a course, e.g. their own back garden or a 'Treasure Island'.

Refer to the course planning section.

BEARING & DISTANCE MEASUREMENT

AGE GROUP	12+
TIME	15-30 min

AIM

• *to practise taking bearings from the map and measuring distances*

EQUIPMENT CHECKLIST

Preparation

Prepare maps by drawing a course on - it may be possible to acquire old pre-marked maps from your local club.

Prepare a master answer card and pupils' test card.

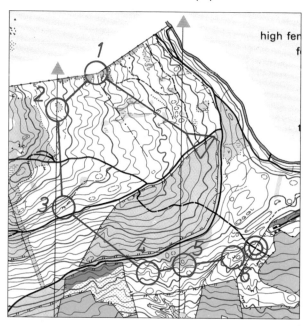

Practical

Pupils have to list bearings and distances for each leg of the course and write a control description for each control.

Alternatively pupils have to fill in the spaces to complete the list of bearings, distances and control descriptions for each leg.

EXAMPLE TEST CARD

	Bearing	Distance	Control Description
S - 1	302°	500m	. . . .
1 - 2	. . . .	225m	Clearing, S tip
2 - 3	177°	. . .	Cliff foot
3 - 4	. . .	. . .	Re-entrant
4 - 5	. . .	150m	Hill
5 - 6	86°	. . .	. . . .
6 - F	. . .	. . .	. . . .

Adaptations and further work

Write down an attack point for each leg then the bearing and distance to the control. This exercise is best practised after teaching several theory sessions - see compass chapter.

Pupils can set each other courses to complete test cards.

COMPASS BEARINGS

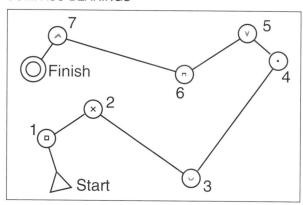

Write down the accurate compass bearing for each leg. Features can be drawn in each circle.

DISTANCE MEASUREMENT

Measure the distance from one control to the next - the centre of each circle.

CONTROL SYMBOL RECOGNITION

See Worksheet 1 (p106).

DESCRIBING A COURSE

AIMS
- *to practise using bearings on a map*
- *to familiarise children with working out routeplans to get round a course*

EQUIPMENT CHECKLIST

Preparation

Plan a course (or several courses). Prepare a card as illustrated for each course.

Have a master map prepared for each course card so that students can check their answers.

EXAMPLE

COURSE CARD

Start	Building		
1 - 2	N. path junction	294°	650m
2 - 3	Spur	42°	350
3 - 4	Path junction	4°	300
4 - 5	Depression	267°	625
5 - 6	Ditch junction	212°	230
6 - 7	Path end	178°	600
7 - 8	Clearing, SE corner	124°	350
8 - 9	Re-entrant (in trees)	90°	350
Finish at Building		54°	150

Practical

Pupils have a blank map showing the position of the start and finish only.

They have to use a compass to work out the bearings and distances on the course card and to plot the course on their map.

Different course cards can be used to make a variety of courses on the same or different maps.

Adaptations and further work

Pupils can draw on the map the route they would take if they were to run the course.

They could annotate this route showing possible attack points, collecting features, even sections where rough orienteering is used and sections where fine orienteering is more appropriate.

They could write a description of how they would get round the course.

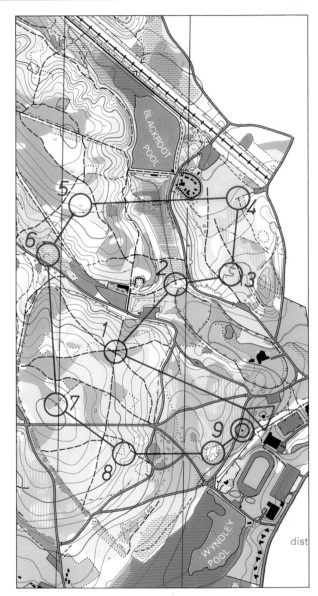

They could make up course cards for each other to work out:

Working in pairs plan one course each. One describes orally the position of the first control, the other tries to plot it on the map. Continue round the course changing over after each control or at the end of the course.

DRAWING PROFILES

AGE GROUP	13+
TIME	30 min+

AIM
• *to encourage a deeper understanding of contours*

EQUIPMENT CHECKLIST

Preparation

Draw a course on a map. Use a map with enough contour detail to make the exercise worthwhile.

Practical

Pupils have to draw a profile of the course as follows.

Use a strip of paper and put it along the line between the controls.

Mark a line on the paper every time a contour is crossed, indicating whether you are climbing or descending.

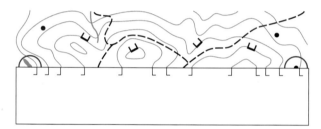

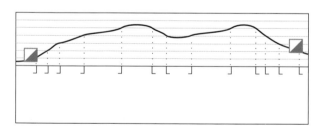

Draw a base line and put the strip of paper along it. Mark the position of the contours above the base line on a vertical scale (1mm - 5m).

Scale is not important at first, as long as an indication of ground shape is produced.

Adaptations and further work

Pupils could draw scaled profiles of a complete course.

Pupils could draw the profile of a route round a course. This has the added complication of bending the paper strip to fit the route. This creates a "profile" of the optimum route.

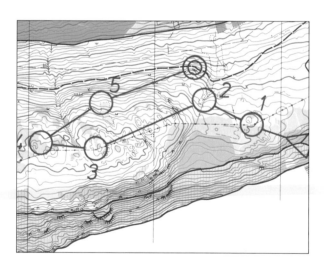

Profile of the course above

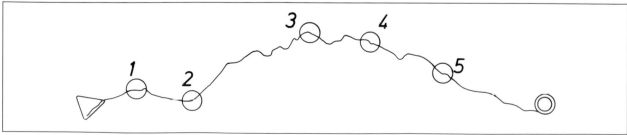

WORD SEARCH

AIM
• to familiarise children with orienteering terminology

EQUIPMENT CHECKLIST

Preparation

Compile lists of words/terms related to orienteering.
Prepare a word search as in the example.

Practical

Children search the box matching words under headings with those in the box. A word may be located horizontally, vertically or diagonally, and in addition from left to right.

CONTROL FEATURES	EQUIPMENT	OTHERS
Contours	Pins	White Rose
Depression	Whistle	Mammoth
Re-entrant	Compass	Start
Knoll	Pen	Finish
Pit	Shoes	Results
Fight	Map case	Prizegiving
Walk	Trophy	Run in
Marsh	Control card	Master
Pond	Punch	Maps
Crag		Taped route
Boulder		Mud
Ditch		Cut
Stream		Tree
Wall		Relay
Path		Winner
Track		Event

Adaptations and further work

Children make up their own word searches.

After completing the search compose a sentence about orienteering.

WORKSHEET 1

AGE GROUP 7+
TIME 10 min +

AIM
* *to evaluate and improve knowledge of orienteering map symbols*

EQUIPMENT CHECKLIST
worksheets

1 Feature identification

Feature	Name		Name	Draw feature
□			Path	
▬			Wall	
– – –			Boulder	
•			Cliff	
etc.			etc.	
. . . .			. . . .	
. . . .			. . . .	
. . . .			. . . .	
. . . .			. . . .	

2 Identify the symbols

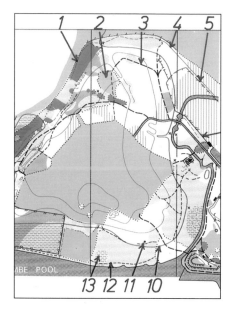

3 Spot the difference. The control sites on the two maps are slightly different.

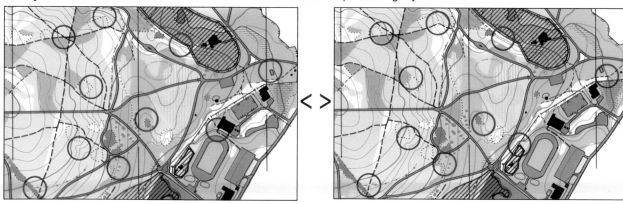

4 Teams of 2

Each pair has a different map with 6 control circles on very distinctive map symbols. They take it in turns to identify and write down the symbols. Maps, which should be numbered, can then be changed over. Use as a running game with a map at one side of the hall or playground, paper and pencil at the other side. Use a variety of full size maps to show a contrast of styles and types of terrain. Do not cut off the legend.

Further work

O bingo, card games, shake a dice to draw a map also test feature identification.

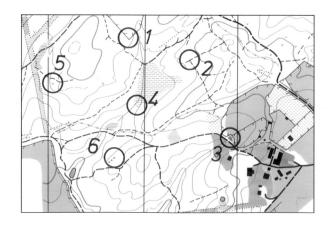

WORKSHEET 2

AIM
* *to evaluate knowledge of skills which have been taught*

EQUIPMENT CHECKLIST
worksheets

Multiple choice - orienteering terms

1 ROUTE CHOICE
   a Finding your way to the event
   b Finding possible routes between controls
   c Finding your best route between controls

2 HANDRAIL
   a A compulsory crossing point
   b A line feature easy to identify and follow
   c A control on a fence or wall

3 COLLECTING FEATURE
   a A large easy feature assisting fast navigation
   b A feature in a group of similar features
   c The largest feature near to a control

4 MAP MEMORY
   a Remembering all the events you have been to
   b Remembering your route to mark on the map at the end of a race
   c Making a mental picture of part of the map

Make up more questions of your own.

Contours

Up, Down,
Along or Over?

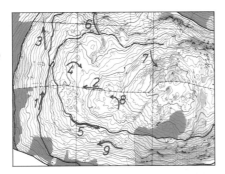

Direction

Write down in which direction you are travelling and what feature you are following.

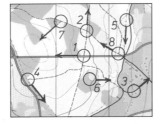

Route Choice

"Which way do I go?" Make up cards each with a map and two controls sharing route choice options. Use these as a basis for discussion.

Contours

Match the profiles with the contours.

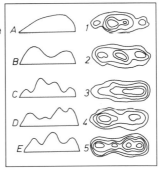

Contours

Match the contours with the description.
A Has steep Southern slopes
B Has steep Northern and Eastern slopes
C Has two summits, the Western one higher
D Is a perfectly even-shaped conical hill
E Has two summits, the Northern one higher

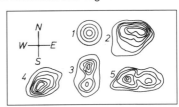

Direction

Make up sets of cards with the eight major directions marked so that everyone in the group has one. Indicate which side of a hall or playground is North. Run around swopping cards at frequent intervals. When the whistle goes each person runs to the corner or side indicated on the card they are holding. The last one into the right place loses a 'life'.

Use a compass - any type of compass can be used.

On the other side of each card draw two controls and a North arrow, with the leg in the same direction as that indicated on side one. When the whistle goes, place the edge of the compass beside the line of the 'leg', set the card with needle to North and run to the right area.

Controls on pieces of map could be used as a progression from this.

9

OUTDOOR ALTERNATIVES

Navigation is fun and the more variety the better. This section provides a few ideas and scope for further work.

STREET ORIENTEERING

AIMS
- *to practise map setting*
- *to develop control flow*

EQUIPMENT CHECKLIST
answer cards

Preparation

Prepare or buy a simple street map of the area to be used. Record the location of fire hydrants, lampposts or any other features which could act as controls, together with any identification numbers or letters (the answers).

Select a number of these points and draw up a master map, allocating numbers to the controls. Put a dot in the centre of each circle precisely where the hydrant/post will be found.

Photocopy the map and colour each circle with a highlighting pen. This is especially useful for a night event.

Prepare an answer card separately.

<u>Ensure that children are not in any danger from busy traffic. Avoid rush hours or poor light.</u>

Practical

Tell everyone what the controls are and what answer is to be looked for.

The answer card is best pinned to clothing together with a pencil on a string. This allows the map to be read more conveniently.

Set pupils off to find the controls and write down the answers (timed or not).

Adaptations and other work

Get pupils to plan question cards for each other.

A variation is not to have a specific feature at a control site. Rather a question to be answered, e.g. date of building, name of bridge builder, etc.

Line, point to point, relay, score orienteering can be planned in such an area.

Street maps without street names are appropriate for more experienced orienteers.

BIKE ORIENTEERING

This same exercise can be done on bikes. It is particularly suitable in a country park with many traffic free roads and paths. It encourages the development of map memory as it is difficult to read a map whilst cycling.

See p111.

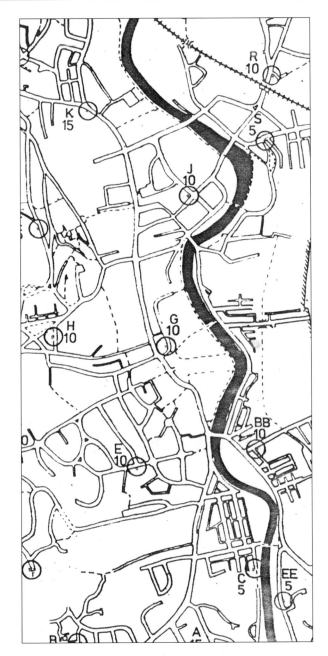

MOUNTAIN ORIENTEERING

AGE GROUP · 17+
TIME · 1 day

AIM
* *to prepare pupils for navigation in mountain areas*

EQUIPMENT CHECKLIST

It is frequently recorded in outdoor centres and camps that the days remembered and enjoyed most are those of the independent walk. For this kind of activity it is recommended that pupils work at least in pairs or groups of 4.

Preparation

Choose a low level hilly area which is not too exposed or dangerous (preferably below 1500ft - above this groups should be supervised by a leader - preferably holding a Mountain Leadership Certificate).

Prepare a course and description sheet giving descriptions, grid references and code letters on controls.

Plan well within the ability level of the group. Public footpaths can be the most confusing features to follow.

Practical

All students must be well briefed about the possible dangers.

Each team must carry compass, map, torch, whistle, bivybag, rucksack, waterproof clothing for every team member, some spare food, e.g. chocolate.

Each team must be sure of safety procedures.

It is useful to have extra staff to shadow teams.

With less experienced students have a member of staff with each team.

Students receive a control description list. Work out the location of the controls and set off at a timed start.

On completion they are timed in and their time for the course is calculated.

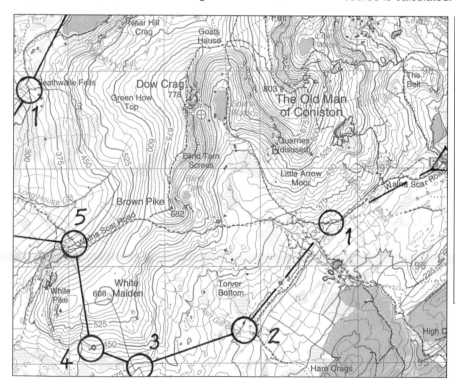

MOUNTAIN ORIENTEERING	
Start	Road end
1	Track junction
2	Stream bend
3	Wall corner
4	Quarry ruin
5	Road/track junction
Camp	Turner Hall Farm
1	Track end
2	Track/wall crossing
3	Footbridge
4	Stream junction
5	Stream/path crossing
6	Lake outlet
Finish	School

Section of a mountain orienteering course. Map scale 1:40,000.
© Harvey Map Services.

Adaptations and further work

This can be made into an expedition - students carrying tents and camping out overnight.

Use this procedure when taking groups on a hill walk. Let each pupil take a turn at finding the route.

Instead of using markers ask questions at each point, e.g. what sort of tree stands 10m north of the ruin?

Discuss events such as the Karrimor International Mountain Marathon.

MOUNTAIN BIKE ORIENTEERING

AIM
• to practise navigation at speed

EQUIPMENT CHECKLIST

There is an increasing interest in the sport of orienteering on mountain bikes. All terrain bikes are used in areas with a rich network of forest trails, tracks, bridleways and 'green roads'.

In Britain the events are often score orienteering competitions over 1, 2 or 5 hours known as Trailquest. Elsewhere point to point courses are usual. The sport is well developed in France, Spain, UK and Czech Republic.

A key restriction in mountain bike orienteering is that participants must keep to tracks and paths throughout the competition. This is particularly important for environmental reasons.

The map shows the speed of a path or track using green lines or dashes (solid line - fast; dashed line - slower).

SKI ORIENTEERING

AIM
• to combine navigation with skill on skis

EQUIPMENT CHECKLIST

The Nordic countries were the birthplace of ski orienteering back at the end of the nineteen century. Now it is well established in Northern and Central Europe, North America and Japan. It has its own World Championships in individual (classic and short distance) and relay.

Like foot orienteering and mountain bike orienteering, the world governing body of ski orienteering is the International Orienteering Federation.

Many ski tracks are prepared in the area using snow scooters. Without pre-made tracks the competition would be unfair with early starters making tracks for others to follow! The tracks are overprinted onto the map in green.

The orienteering problems are more of route choice than in finding the controls.

TREASURE HUNT

AIMS

- *to show an alternative way of using maps and map reading skills*
- *to involve pupils in decision making and problem solving*

EQUIPMENT CHECKLIST

Preparation

The example below is one of many variations which can be developed. Read through the example and adapt the exercise for your own maps. When planning always start with the final 'treasure' hiding place and work backwards, as shown in the example below.

1 Final hiding place - the lake at grid ref. 327050.

2 Work out a code (e.g. A = 0, B = 1, etc.). Put the grid reference of the hiding place into code (327050 = DCHAFA).

3 Work out 6 places to hang markers in the area. Each marker will carry one of the code letters.

4 Prepare the initial CLUE SHEET.

5 Prepare a CODE BREAKER SHEET and final clue.

Practical

Divide pupils into equal groups of 4-8.

Give each group the CLUE SHEET and get them to work out the location of the 6 markers.

The group can then divide up to find the markers and write down the code letters.

They return to base and receive the CODE BREAKER SHEET and final clue.

The grid reference has to be worked out using the code breaker and then the final clue to decide exactly where the 'treasure' is.

They go and find the treasure. In this case it is in the lake - suspended 2 feet underwater - but you could choose an easier site!

CLUE SHEET

Find markers at these 6 places and note down the code letter at each one (the group can split up).

1 315034 Little Langdale School
2 336052 High Close YHA Gate
3 322055 Chapel Stile Church
4 314049 Thrang Farm Gate
5 344034 Skelwith Bridge Cafe
6 330031 Colwith Farm

CODE BREAKER

Convert the letters of your answer to numbers using the following code :
A=0, B=1, C=2, D=3, etc. This gives you the grid reference of the final hiding place.

FINAL CLUE: 60cm (2 feet) under!

Contour (15m interval)
Index contour (75m interval)

Adaptations and further work

Endless!

Instead of using markers, ask questions about the places (Q1: What colour is the cottage door? A1: Red). In the code breaker sheet use A = O, B = 1, etc. and say the second letter in answer 1 converts to the first number in the grid reference (E = 4).

These exercises can be used on any scale of map (e.g. 1:50,000 or 1:25,000). With clues about 2km from base, the exercise takes about half a day. Longer distances or more clues would take longer. Exercises could last several days and be combined with camping.

BOAT - SAIL - CANOE ORIENTEERING

AIMS
- *to provide some variety for students who already have experience with boats*
- *to spice up a sailing or canoeing day at an outdoor centre*
- *to introduce outdoor enthusiasts in these sports to orienteering*

EQUIPMENT CHECKLIST

Preparation and practical

Prepare a course and control description sheet as shown. Buoys and other mid water obstacles could be used.

Run the event just as any other orienteering session, i.e. set out course, punch a master card.

Students set out at 2-5 minute intervals and are timed around the course. This course could be used in either direction (1-7 or 7-1).

If visibility is very good a score event might be more suitable than a point to point course. Alternatively plan a separate course for each boat.

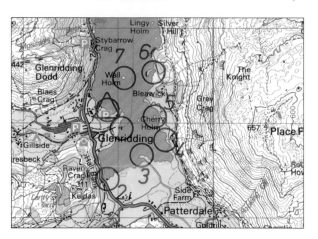

Adaptations and further work

This theme is capable of expansion but care must be taken not to break any safety codes associated with such activities.

CONTROL DESCRIPTIONS

1 Jetty, N. tip

2 Building, W. side

3 Peninsular tip

4 Outlet

5 Island, N. tip

6 Inlet

7 Island, W. side

TEAM CHALLENGE

AGE GROUP	adults
TIME	2 hrs

AIM
- to design orienteering/navigation exercises that are part of team building and outdoor challenge programmes

EQUIPMENT CHECKLIST
rope, canoes, helmets, life jackets

Outdoor pursuits feature strongly in programmes of activities designed to encourage team building.

Management techniques, i.e. planning, communication, time management, co-ordination, decision making and evaluation are developed using a graded series of problem solving activities. The objective is to use outdoor challenges to help people to:

- take responsibility for their own learning,

- share their learning with others,

- have fun.

Preparation

The navigation example below is one of many that can be developed.

Decide on the most suitable area and if possible use a coloured map.

The objective is for teams to achieve the greatest score within a time limit with points deducted for late return. Each team must divide up the controls taking into account individuals' fitness and navigational ability.

Draw up master maps for each team and a description sheet.

Adaptations

There are many possibilities depending upon the time available, the nature of the group and the equipment available.

- A point to point course with instructions at each control of a technical nature related to work.

- The exercise might include a journey over water by raft which needs to be built using barrels, planks and rope. The safety aspects are very important in such an exercise.

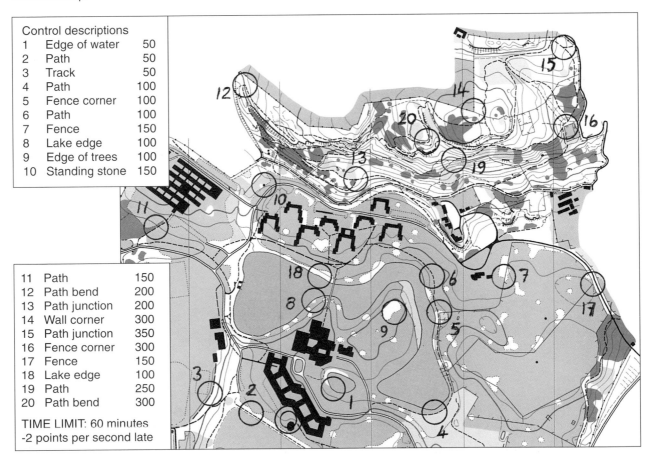

Control descriptions

1	Edge of water	50
2	Path	50
3	Track	50
4	Path	100
5	Fence corner	100
6	Path	100
7	Fence	150
8	Lake edge	100
9	Edge of trees	100
10	Standing stone	150

11	Path	150
12	Path bend	200
13	Path junction	200
14	Wall corner	300
15	Path junction	350
16	Fence corner	300
17	Fence	150
18	Lake edge	100
19	Path	250
20	Path bend	300

TIME LIMIT: 60 minutes
-2 points per second late

10

PHYSICAL AND MENTAL FITNESS

In recent years there has been an increase in awareness by the general population of the importance of physical fitness and its relation to healthy living. Teachers and coaches working with young children have a major role to play in encouraging children to adopt a physically active lifestyle throughout life. Health related physical fitness has become a priority in our society. The sport of orienteering, well known for its appeal to a wide age range, its emphasis on running and the healthy outdoor life, offers an attractive vehicle for the promotion of fitness through participation.

The planning of training schedules and fitness sessions are fully explained in the British Orienteering Federation's Training and Coaching manual. This selection of exercises offers ideas for incorporating map games and technique practice into what are primarily fitness sessions.

INDOOR EXERCISES

AIMS
* *to improve cardiovascular endurance*
* *to improve map memory*

AGE GROUP
TIME **15-30min**

EQUIPMENT CHECKLIST
1: matching map pieces
2: cards, map jigsaws, blank maps + masters

EXERCISE 1 (Indoors or Outdoors)

Preparation

Obtain a supply of orienteering maps and cut out pairs of identical map pieces, approximately 25mm (1") square, to form two identical sets. If possible mount the sets on differently coloured card.

Letter one set (A - B - C - D -) and number the other set randomly.

Lay out the sets on separate benches a good distance apart.

Lesson

Line the children up between the benches, each having paper and a pencil.

On the whistle the children run backwards and for-wards matching the map pieces and identifying letters with numbers. The answers are written down on the paper left in the centre.

The winner is the first person to complete the task with all answers correct.

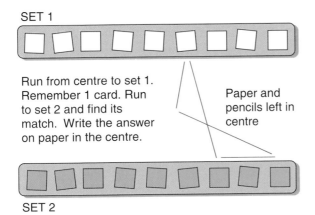

SET 1

Run from centre to set 1. Remember 1 card. Run to set 2 and find its match. Write the answer on paper in the centre.

Paper and pencils left in centre

SET 2

Adaptations

Increase the distance between the cards.

Increase the number of cards per set.

Increase the difficulty e.g. contour only maps.

Use the exercise outdoors, say bottom and top of a hill or at the front and back of the school.

EXERCISE 2 (Indoors)

Preparation

Set up circuit and tasks (see diagram).

Lesson

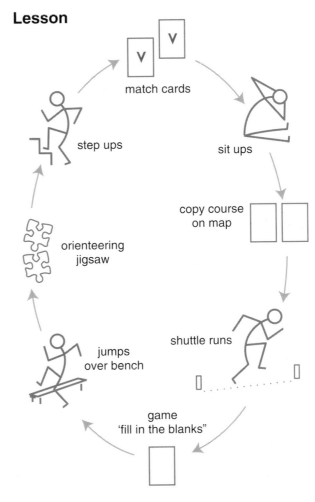

match cards

sit ups

copy course on map

shuttle runs

game 'fill in the blanks"

jumps over bench

orienteering jigsaw

step ups

Adaptations

The number of exercises at each station can be increased.

The orienteering task difficulty can be extended.

Children could work in pairs - one recording, the other working.

Other games which can be used include 'Fill in the blanks' (p96) or 'Memory games' (p97).

OUTDOOR EXERCISES

AIMS
- *to improve cardiovascular endurance*
- *to practise orienteering skills*

AGE GROUP

TIME 15-30min

EQUIPMENT CHECKLIST

Exercise 1

HANGING/RETRIEVING MARKERS

Prepare master maps. Mark a number of controls and a central start. Divide children into pairs.

One member of each pair runs to a (different) control site, hangs a micro marker and returns. They pass the marked map to their partner who runs to the control and returns with it.

They then continue until all the controls have been hung/retrieved.

Alternate the hanging/retrieving.

Children less than 15 years of age should achieve fitness mostly through fun activities and competition. We would certainly not recommend a heavy physical programme of road running.

A typical week for a 14 year old would at most be:

Monday	Rest
Tuesday	Indoor session or alternative sport e.g. Badminton
Wednesday	Technique practice and short run in woodland
Thursday	Rest
Friday	A run through woodland of no more than 3 km (2 miles)
Saturday	Rest
Sunday	Orienteering event

Before undertaking strenuous exercise of any kind the body should be warm and flexible.

Exercise 2

PUNCHING PRACTICE

Using the control card pinned correctly to the chest or arm children run backwards and forwards punching the card until all the boxes are filled.

Only legible punch marks should be counted.

Adaptations

For exercise 2 consider relay races or timed competitions.

Many of the games or playground lessons, e.g. relays, score orienteering or mini map races, mentioned in chapter 3 can be attempted with more emphasis on the physical and less on the technical aspect.

If more serious training is to be undertaken, building up very gradually to continuous running for 60 minutes is a realistic target.

MENTAL FITNESS

AIM
* *to enjoy orienteering through successful application of techniques
  in a competitive situation*

EQUIPMENT CHECKLIST

The 'Thought Sport' or 'Cunning Running', orienteering makes demands on psychological capacities as much as physical fitness.

> Decision making
>
> Concentration
>
> Handling competition nerves
>
> Ignoring distractions
>
> Race preparation
>
> Goal setting

These and other aspects of psychological training are well recorded in the 'Training and Coaching' handbook (BOF 1982). Teachers can introduce some basic principles to their group of juniors or beginners. Young people are often more receptive to new ideas than experienced orienteers.

The objectives here are directed to enjoyment through successfully applying techniques in a race situation; not to the creation of selfish competitors where winning matters most.

GOAL SETTING

What do I want to get out of orienteering?

> Enjoyment?
> Success?
> Days out in the country?
> A gold badge?
> Membership of a squad?

Plan

* Events
* Courses
    - *for success, yellow*
    - *for technical practice, orange*
* Realistic goals
    - *to complete 10 yellow courses without asking for help*
    - *to be within 15 minutes of the winner on all orange courses*
    - *to get a bronze badge in my first year of badge events*
* Technical goals
    - *check every code before I punch*
    - *always plan my route before I run off from a control.*

Record ...

* All event and results in a log book
* Draw routes, estimate time lost
* Why?
    - Complete race analysis sheet (p126)
    - Goal achieved?
    - Did I do what I set out to do?
    - What should I aim for next time?

RACE PREPARATION

The quality of results usually reflect the quality of preparation.

Before

* Where is the event?
* What sort of terrain?
* What techniques will be needed?
* What scale is the map?
* What will the weather be like?
* Do I have to pre-enter?
* Transport? Accommodation?
* Clothing, shoes ready?

On the day

* How far is the start?
* What is the start system?
* Can I see the last control(s)?
* Do I want to chat to people or think about the race on my own?
* Warm up?
* How am I going to orienteer? (What went wrong at the last event?)

Concentration

This is affected by:
* Motivation (goal setting)
* Interest in the event (enjoyment)
* Positive attitude (looking forward to the race)
* Confidence to complete the course and solve problems
* Good preparation
* Being aware of distractions, e.g. seeing someone you know
* Relaxation and nerves

Discuss how these aspects can influence performance in a positive and negative way.

PRACTICAL EXERCISES FOR MENTAL FITNESS

EQUIPMENT CHECKLIST

Think positively

- *I can get round on my own and find all the controls.*

- *I'm not going to make any mistakes today.*

- *If I get lost, I'm going to find myself and not panic.*

- *I'm going to go out and do my best.*

Picture yourself orienteering well

Simple imagery techniques can be introduced to youngsters as part of a positive approach towards improvement, as a PE teacher might use in a gymnastics lesson.

- *Sit quietly and still (!!), close your eyes and imagine yourself orienteering. This is always more effective when relaxed.*

- *Picture yourself planning your route and reading the map carefully to the first control - feeling excited but calm.*

- *Visualise running fluently and reading the map at the same time.*

- *See yourself punching at a control and moving away quickly in the right direction.*

- *Imagine meeting someone you know and not being distracted.*

Relax

Learn to be in control of yourself, your body and your nerves. Use some appropriate background music:

- Lie or sit down comfortably.

- Observe your own breathing and make it deeper.

- Feel the contrast between having a muscle tense and then relaxed - work through the body, not forgetting your eyes and face.

- Feel heavy, warm, relaxed, calm.

At the next event

Spend 5 minutes relaxing and thinking about how you are going to orienteer.

ENJOY YOURSELF.

11

ORIENTEERING PROGRAMMES IN EDUCATION

Orienteering has been described in various ways during its relatively short history as a sport -

> 'Competitive navigation on foot'
>
> 'Cunning Running'
>
> 'The Thought Sport'

The implication is of course that the sport has a unique blend of mental and physical skills that must be developed by the successful competitor.

When the activity is introduced and taught to young-sters as this book suggests via the classroom, the school fields and the forest, they will rapidly achieve the necessary mental and physical skills. They will enjoy its challenges and they will relish the excitement that successful navigation brings.

The physical and mental challenges will be real 'experiences' for children and it should not be too difficult to use these experiences to persuade children to talk about them, to write about them or to tackle problems that have been previously attempted in other, perhaps more traditional ways.

The intention then, is to use the children's experiences as they participate in the sport to stimulate work across the curriculum. Orienteering becomes a 'centre of interest', a 'theme', 'a topic' or a 'learning medium'.

Whereas the Projects might best be suited to the primary teacher, the Modules give a ready-made structure for developing orienteering within the restricted curriculum of a secondary school.

ORIENTEERING IN THE SCHOOL CURRICULUM

Orienteering activities can link areas of the school curriculum together. In particular skills needed in physical education, geography and mathematics can be learnt and practised through learning how to orienteer.

PHYSICAL EDUCATION
Specific requirements:
(i) Athletic activity
(ii) Games
(iii) Outdoor activities
General requirement:
(i) Cross curricular links
(ii) Physical activity

GEOGRAPHY
Geographical skills:
(i) Use of maps
(ii) Fieldwork techniques
Knowledge & understanding of places
Physical geography
Environmental geography

ORIENTEERING

MATHEMATICS
Application of mathematics:
(i) In practical tasks
(ii) Real life problem solving
Number
Shape and space:
(i) Measurement and location in the study of space
Handling data

ENGLISH
Speaking and listening
Writing

The skills of orienteering linked to 4 core subjects

The practical value of map and compass skills is not about learning cardinal points and symbols or grid references for their own sake, but more about learning to relate map and compass to the terrain, to notice features on the ground which can be located on the map and then to reach the control destination as efficiently and quickly as possible. The two vital tools - map and compass - have important applications in fieldwork and the wider outdoor world, while in physical terms walking or running up and down hills or across rough terrain can be an exciting and effective way of building up strength and cardiovascular fitness.

Once the young navigator understands the map and starts to use it, key questions immediately pose themselves centring round 5 important areas - orientation, location, route choice, map content and speed of progress. Here are some examples:

ORIENTATION
Is the map the right way round?
Does the map match the ground?
How do I use the compass to set the map?

LOCATION
Where am I now?

Can I find this point on the map?

ROUTE CHOICE
Where am I going?
Which are the best ways to get there?
Which is the shortest route?
Are there any obstacles in the way?
Which route is the easiest to follow and to find the control from?
Which route is the best for me?
In which direction do I set off?

MAP CONTENT AND STAYING ON THE ROUTE
What features can I check off to make sure I am going the right way?
How can I keep a check on my position?
How will I know when I am near my destination?

SPEED
Am I making mistakes through getting out of breath and tiredness?
Should I slow down and take more care?
Am I forgetting to use back up techniques like compass and distance judgement through running too fast?
Am I fit enough to last the whole course?

Evaluation also poses important questions which the teacher can draw out from pupils. Because orienteers are often alone or out of sight of the teacher it is important that pupils are guided to assess their performance after every activity. They should be encouraged to swap questions like this with their friends:

How pleased was I with my performance?
How could I do better next time?
Did I find the controls precisely?
If not, where were mistakes made and why?
Did I lose time through being too hesitant or checking the map too often?
Were there quicker routes with less climbing or rough ground?

The answers to these questions contribute to many aspects of the school curriculum. The application of directional skills, the use of map and compass and the identification of features relate directly to geography programmes of study while key concepts like distance, direction, location, shape, scale and networks are shared with mathematics. Finally, after any interesting experience, young people inevitably like to talk to others about it. Recalling and describing routes and assessing performance introduce the communication and language skills of English.

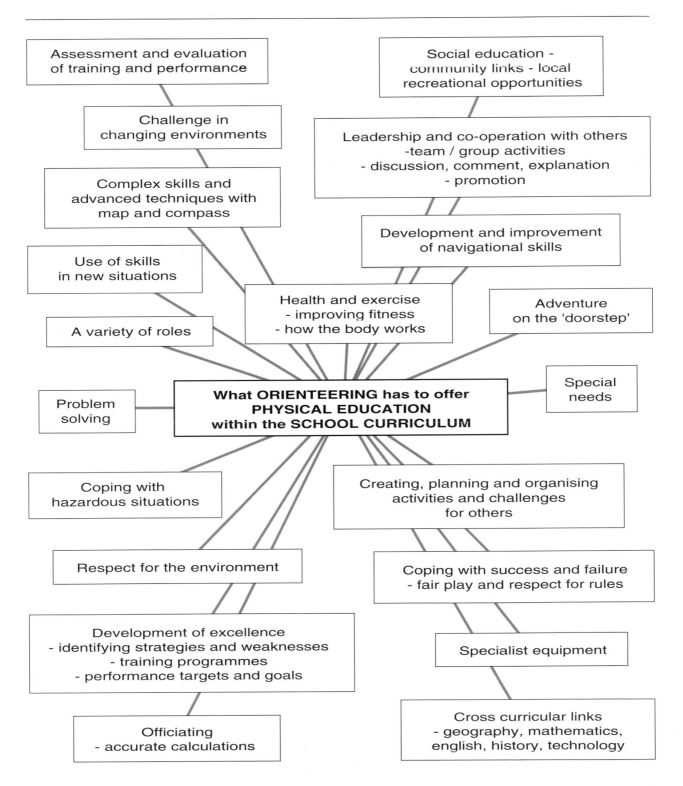

CLASSROOM PROJECT 1

AIM
* *to use orienteering to stimulate classroom work in History, Science, Measurement, Language, Expressive Arts, Health Studies and Geography*

AGE GROUP
TIME   Flexible according to content chosen. Probably to be considered as a medium term project

---

Preparation

HISTORY:
* The "Navigators"
* Romans:
  mile - "mille passus"
  pacing techniques
  latitude/longitude
* Chinese: compass needle
* Vikings: Use of the Pole Star
* Portuguese: astrolabe and cross staff
* Scandinavia - origins of the sport of orienteering

SCIENCE:
* The Norths
  - true, magnetic, grid
* Magnetism
* Climate
* The trees in our forests
* Nature shows the way:
  - prevailing winds shape the direction of trees
  - moss predominates on the north side of stones/trees
  - at noon the sun is due south

MEASUREMENT:
* Timing of races
* Distance estimation
* Scale 1:5000, 1:10 000, 1:15 000 etc.
* Bearings
* Results in graphical form
* Badge scheme times
  - gold, silver, bronze
* Making a plan of the classroom
* Contour intervals
  - estimating the height of a hill
* Speed = Distance/Time
* Compass sectors, angles

LANGUAGE:
* The technical terms of the sport (i.e. handrails, attack points, collecting features, knolls, etc.)
* Experiential discussion
  - how did you complete your course

LANGUAGE (CONT.)
* Use of symbols
* IOF symbols
* Creative writing - explaining your route choice, how you felt
* Your poem "Waiting for the .... (start). Heart .... (pounding) bracketed words taken from a word bank

EXPRESSIVE ARTS:
* Painting, photography, drawing
* Making your own orienteering equipment
* Collage from objects
* Signs
* Symbols
* Posters advertising the School Club
* Markers from plastic juice bottles
* Displaying results
* Creative dance - theme 'Waiting for the whistle' 'Off I go' 'Into the finish', etc.
* Making models from contours

HEALTH STUDIES:
* First aid
* Safety in the forest
* The country code
* Diet
* Self catering out of doors
* Healthy living
* The dangers of smoking

GEOGRAPHY:
* Maps for travel, roads, etc.
* Maps for hillwalking (OS maps, Harvey maps)
* Maps for orienteers
* Use of grid references
* Interpretation of contours
* Scandinavian countries - birthplace of orienteering
* The venues of the World Orienteering Champs - Sweden, Finland, Scotland, Switzerland, Hungary, Australia, etc
* Man at work - the forester, the cartographer

Example

EXPRESSIVE ARTS: MAKING YOUR OWN ORIENTEERING EQUIPMENT

AIMS
* *to supplement the practical orienteering exercises that may be included in the Primary programme.*
* *to provide materials that the children and the teacher can use practically.*
* *to make a contribution to the expressive arts programme in the school.*

EQUIPMENT:
card, red/orange poster paint, clear adhesive plastic film

Practical

1 Make the 15 orienteering markers you will need for the practical course. Use card or hardboard and cut to approx. 20cm square. Colour the shaded part red. Add code numbers1-15 and letters A, B, C etc. in black. Cover in clear adhesive film if using card. Make holes in the corners and thread cord so that the control can hang. Colour and mark both sides of the control.

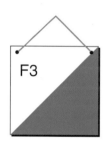

2 Make 10 mini-markers (for use in the classroom). Use paper and cut the markers approx. 5-8cm square. Colour shaded part red. Put removable adhesive on the back of each marker.

3 Draw a simple black and white map of your classroom. See 'Drawing a plan of the classroom' (p19).

4 Design your own control card.

5 Make your own 'punches' from thick wax crayons in different colours. Attach a string for hanging at the control.

CLASSROOM PROJECT 2

AGE GROUP
TIME   Flexible according to the depth undertaken but likely to be a major project probably taking up a school term

AIMS

- *to complete a classroom project on the organisation of a school's orienteering event*
- *to use the event as a catalyst for a wide variety of work across the curriculum*

This approach involves the use of a storyline supplied by the teacher and selection of activities often decided by a question and answer session between the teacher and class.

STORYLINE:	ACTIVITIES:
We have been asked to organise the .... Orienteering Event for all the primary schools in this authority Which schools will participate?	• Why should the class organise this event? • Where should we hold it? • List those schools eligible • List of past participants in orienteering • Co-ordinate with the Outdoor Education Advisor in writing
What facilities are needed?	• Suitable terrain • Changing facilities • Car/minibus parking • Start/finish areas
How is the event to be organised?	• Committees are appointed by the class teacher • Advertise for tenders
The event needs a motif - brochure, posters, car stickers, pennants etc. Why?	• Competition for the design of the advertising materials • Investigate the historical development of orienteering to capture the tradition • Consult sponsor re. advertising, production of stickers etc.
Build up a plan of the area chosen (country park, historic house). Visit the park and survey it for suitability - look for start/finish/spectator areas etc.	• Use boxes, cord etc. to construct a model of the site • Develop the history of the country park and historic building • Arrange for a guided tour by the custodians
We need to commission a competition song and perhaps an opening speech.	• Compose a song, perhaps an existing song but new words • Prepare a speech to welcome competitors
How will the competitors arrive?	• Discuss the location of the schools that will take part • What are the travel possibilities? • What alternatives? • What are the travel timetables?
How much will the event cost to run?	• How much do we charge competitors to compete? • How do we collect money? • What do we do with it initially? • What do we do with any profit? • What services can the local bank offer? • How do we keep accounts?
Who do we ask for permission to run the event?	• Letters to the orienteering fixtures secretary • Letters to the local club • Can an experienced orienteer visit the school to advise us?
All large sporting events need an Official Programme.	• Design and produce a programme which gives all necessary information to teachers/pupils
What courses do we have to have for this school's event?	• Design courses both in classroom and externally • Draw up a list of equipment needed • Design and make what we don't have - banners, punches ...
How do we know our courses are suitable? How are we going to open the event?	• Involve a local orienteering club; ask them for a controller • Invite a personality to perform the ceremony/award prizes • Use a video camera for the school news programme • Provide interviews for the local radio station
On the day participation will need to be carefully thought out.	• Take all children involved in this event to participate in a real event to clarify their thinking before the big day • Run the event on the day using start team/finish team/first aid/car parking/putting out and collecting controls/results team - collate and display results

Adaptations and further work

A project of this size provides opportunity for many follow-up activities:
- *writing thank-you letters*
- *writing about the day of the event*

- *graphically displaying the results*
- *researching colour coded courses and other events*
- *making contour models*
- *editing film material, radio interviews*

CLASSROOM PROJECT 3
Keeping a log book

AIMS
• to provide a reference point for individual recall of work done on orienteering
• to establish a routine of recording routes and results as a means of evaluating performance

EQUIPMENT CHECKLIST
folder, files

LOG BOOK THEORY

Select from the list below to support the practical exercises completed:

1   Orienteering - what is it? Decorate folder. Draw or sketch someone orienteering.

2   Classroom or playground maps. Write about scale, symbols, types of orienteering. 'How I feel about orienteering'. Poem.

3   Make a game using the local map, e.g. jigsaw (p94), fill in the blanks (p96) or other games such as wordsearch (p105).

4   Draw a 'treasure island' map (p99).

5   Orienteering map symbols. Divide them according to colour or line/point features. Select the symbols used in the lesson.

6   Notes on theory lessons (chapters 6 and 7).

7   A course planning exercise (p101).

8   Worksheets on orienteering (p106,107)

9   A glossary of orienteering words.

Further work

Use your own or pupils' ideas. Refer to p124,125.

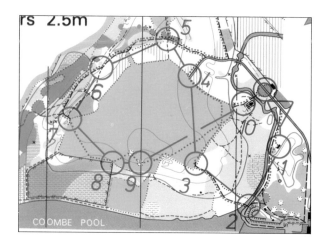

EVENT LOG: ORIENTEERING EVENT ANALYSIS AND EVALUATION

Event	Schools League
Course	Yellow
Date	March 1997
Length	1.8km

MY TIME   30.15   WINNER   19.30
Min / km   Min / km
Total time lost 12 minutes

Summary of mistakes:

Leg	What went wrong and why:	Est. time lost
3-4	Played safe and followed edges of trees instead of cutting across.	1 min.
5-6	Saw Ann behind me and rushed off the wrong way, finished up on the road, took me ages to work out where I was.	10 min.
8-9	Went to the wrong tree first of all. Control fallen on to ground.	1 min.

Strengths (What went right today?):

Ran well. I'm good at thumbing the map now. Sorted myself out after getting lost going to 6.

Weaknesses and lessons learnt:

Kept stopping a lot but didn't stop to think - just ran off.

Other comments:

Enjoyed doing it on my own. Saw a squirrel. Might try running once or twice a week.

LOOK AT THIS SHEET BEFORE YOUR NEXT EVENT.

MODULES 1

Increasing use is being made in schools and colleges, of programmes of study that are made up of modules, usually of 40 hours duration. An essential and desirable feature of nationally devised and approved modules is a statement of the learning outcomes, i.e. a statement of what the student is able to do. The following examples have been constructed and are in use with secondary children age 12-16 years and intended for use as part of the school's physical education programme.

Title

ORIENTEERING GENERAL COURSE

Type and Purpose

A general course suitable for those with an interest in/ aptitude for running or navigation.

It aims to provide a knowledge and understanding of the sport and to provide sufficient practical expertise to compete in a club level orienteering event.

Preferred Entry Level

Completion of a fitness/health course.

Completion of a sample course in outdoor education.

Learning Outcomes

The student should:

1/ Be aware of the structure of the National Orienteering Association/Federation and the competitions it runs.

2/ Understand the fundamentals of basic navigational techniques.

3/ Complete effectively courses set at 'yellow/orange' level (or equivalent) in the colour coded scheme.

4/ Achieve a fitness level necessary to compete effectively.

Content or Context

1/ Historical development of the sport.

2/ The nature and effectiveness of the National Orienteering Federation in running the sport.

3/ Forms of competition.

4/ Training techniques and programmes to improve fitness levels.

5/ Self monitoring of the above.

6/ Basic techniques:

(i) map orientation (setting).

(ii) map familiarisation including relationship between map and terrain.

(iii) basic understanding of contours.

(iv) rough orienteering techniques, i.e. hand-rails.

(v) using the compass.

(vi) distance estimation techniques.

(vii) competitive techniques, i.e. master map procedure, description sheet, control flow.

Suggested Learning and Teaching Approaches

The module provides a basic introduction to the sport and develops students' knowledge of the structure and skills.

Teaching approaches can include:

1/ Formal class lectures using audio visual packages, cassettes, slide presentations.

2/ Practical sessions based in and out of school.

3/ Competition at one of the Galoppen (schools) events.

Assessment Procedures

1/ Students keep a log book showing

(i) tasks set using any audio visual resources/ worksheets that are available.

(ii) practical work undertaken to include an evaluation (self monitoring) of their own performance.

2/ Students will achieve a practical standard based on the colour coding system in operation at orienteering events.

References and Resources

See p153.

MODULES 2

ORIENTEERING PROGRAMMES IN EDUCATION

Title

ORIENTEERING A

Type and Purpose

A specialist module for advanced performers. Suitable for those who performed ably in the general course and who wish to pursue practical expertise in order to compete in badge standard events.

Preferred Entry Level

To have successfully completed the general course.

Learning Outcomes

The student should:

1/ Be familiar with the structure of the sport as run by the National Federation and understand the incentive schemes.

2/ Further develop navigational skills in order to complete courses of badge standard.

3/ Plan and carry out a fitness programme designed to support navigational techniques.

4/ Self monitor such a programme.

5/ Achieve a bronze level badge of the National Badge scheme.

Content/Context

1/ The structure of the National Federation - the Badge schemes - the junior orienteering scene nationally including the district squads.

2/ The development of sound navigational techniques:

- rough and fine orienteering

- compass skills

- estimation of distance across different terrains

- pre-planning whilst using a handrail

- control flow

- using contour-only maps

3/ The development of a running programme and its link to major events.

Suggested Learning and Teaching Approaches

The module extends the pupils' understanding and further develops basic techniques.

Teaching approaches will include:

1/ Formal class lectures.

2/ Small group practical sessions.

3/ Participation in a variety of orienteering events, e.g. cross country, score, relay, night.

Assessment Procedures

Students will keep a log book showing

a/ tasks set using any resources/worksheets that are available

b/ practical work undertaken to include an evaluation (self-monitoring) of their own performance.

Students will achieve a practical standard based on the bronze, silver and gold awards of the National badge scheme.

References

See p153.

MODULES 3

Title
ORIENTEERING B

Type and Purpose
A specialist module for students who wish to become involved with the administration of the sport and its development.

Preferred Entry Level
To have successfully completed the general course.

Learning Outcomes
The student should:

1/ Be familiar with the organisation and administration necessary in order to run an orienteering event.

2/ Understand the principles involved in course planning.

3/ Understand the duties undertaken by the controller.

4/ Organise and plan a point to point course for younger pupils.

5/ Act as controller for events planned and organised by other pupils.

6/ Complete a black and white orienteering map of school grounds.

7/ Demonstrate an ability to cope with any injuries of a minor nature that occur in the sport.

Content/Context

1/ Introduction to the procedure involved for an average competitor, from entry to course completion.

2/ Introduction to course planning principles and procedures.

3/ Introduction to the duties involved in controlling an orienteering event.

4/ Introduction to map making:

    (i) use of a base map

    (ii) surveying techniques

    (iii) drawing techniques

5/ Application of basic first aid techniques to injured orienteers.

Suggested Learning and Teaching Approaches

1/ Formal lectures.

2/ Field studies necessary for map making.

3/ Use of outside speakers (controllers, course planners).

4/ Practical first aid course.

Assessment Procedures

1/ Observation of performances during the running of an orienteering event for younger pupils.

2/ Analysis of course planning tasks set.

3/ Practical use by other orienteers of the prepared map.

4/ Written paper on first aid and safety procedures.

References
B.O.F. Course Planning.

Harvey 'Mapmaking for Orienteers'.

B.O.F. Rules and Guidelines.

12

PLANNING, ORGANISATION & RULES

Planning and organising a successful competition can be the most satisfying aspect of teaching orienteering. The aim is to create fair courses which everyone completes and enjoys within a framework which offers accurate timing and allows the beginner to follow the system with minimum confusion.

The most important aspect is to get every control hung in the right place but as organiser you are expected to have thought of everything from an unexpected downpour of rain, the start clock packing up, cows in the finish field and a bus load of beginners arriving just as you run out of control descriptions.

The section offers guidelines for you or your students to plan and organise a small orienteering competition. Experienced organisers should also find the checklist useful. For further information on planning and event organisation contact the orienteering federation (p153).

COURSE PLANNING PRINCIPLES

AIMS
- *to plan a course to teach/test orienteering skills*
- *to enable everyone to complete the course*
- *to develop individual's confidence in making independent decisions*

EQUIPMENT CHECKLIST
stencils, measuring string

- <u>A course can never be too easy for young beginners.</u>

- Controls are reassuring - beginners need lots of controls linked by distinctive line features.

- Plan at the correct technical standard (see p132)

- The start must be located on a distinctive feature (on map and ground).

- All control points must be on precise map and ground features.

- The control site must correspond with the centre of a red circle 5-6 mm in diameter.

- Controls should be seen if approached from any direction, never hidden in bushes or behind a tree.

- The presence of other people at a control should not make a significant difference to its visibility.

Select the size of marker to suit the terrain:

5 cm square - classroom
10 cm square - school grounds
20 cm square - parks
30 cm square - woodland

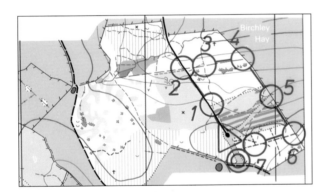

- Vary the length of legs and control features in point to point orienteering.

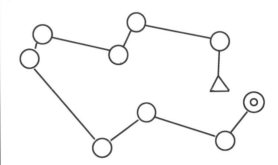

In score orienteering, controls should be evenly distributed and easy to find. There should be plenty of controls near the start.

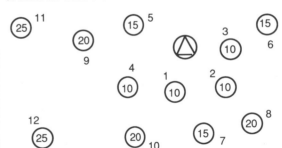

Do not group high scoring controls together. Number controls to discourage visiting them in order 1-15.

- Avoid 'dog legs' - going in and coming out of a control the same way.

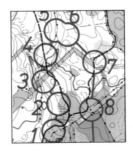
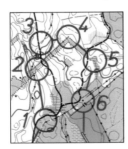

This course is full of dog legs for the competitors choosing to follow the main track 1-2, 2-3, 5-6 and wide ride 3-4. These can usually be avoided by adjusting the position of some controls or adding new controls.

- Avoid 'impossible' or dangerous legs

- unfair to tempt people through 'impossible' green

- quarry dangerous if approached from above.

COLOUR CODED COURSES

AGE GROUP
TIME

AIMS
- *to offer clear standards for a limited range of courses*
- *to serve as a guideline for competitor and planner*

EQUIPMENT CHECKLIST

Colour coded courses are usually used for school leagues and club events. They provide an excellent guide for the planner and competitor alike and offer logical progressions of technical standard for the enthusiastic novice. The teacher of novices will be concerned with developing experience within the white then yellow range of courses, planning to gradually introduce the variety of line features and vegetation then creating opportunities for simple route choice decision making.

WHITE AND YELLOW

A series of white - yellow courses introducing line features and vegetation changes.

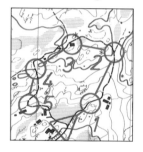
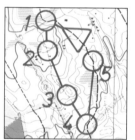
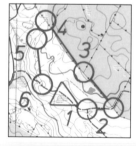

Completing 15-20 yellow standard courses is a good guide. The skills of reading the map on the run and control flow can be developed if a pupil is finding 'yellow' too easy. Juniors aged 9-15 can progress quite quickly to orange standard courses with good instruction and plenty of successful decision making experience to develop confidence.

ORANGE

"Which way shall I go?"
- Controls on line features or large point features.
- Route choice must include handrails. Where this is not possible controls should be within 150 metres of a handrail or leg length should not exceed 150m.
- Controls should be found without the necessity of fine compass, fine contour interpretation or precise distance judgement.

COLOUR CODED COURSES (BRITAIN)

Colour	Length	Tech	Control site	Type of leg	Time	Age
STRING	<0.8km	Easy	On the line		10min	3-10
WHITE	1-1.5	V. easy	Major line features + junctions	Line features No route choice	15-40	6-12
YELLOW	1-2.5	Easy	Line features + very easy adjacent features	Line features Minimal route choice No compass	20-45	8+
ORANGE	2-3.5	Medium	Minor line + easy point features	Route choice Collecting features	35-55	10+ adult novice
RED	4.5-6	Medium			50-80	
LIGHT GREEN	3-4	Med/hard	Minor line + easy point features	Good relocating features near control	35-60	
GREEN	3.5-4.5	Hard	Small point + contours	Fine compass and contours More physical	35-55	
BLUE	4.5-6.5	Hard			50-75	
BROWN	6.5+	Hard			60-85	

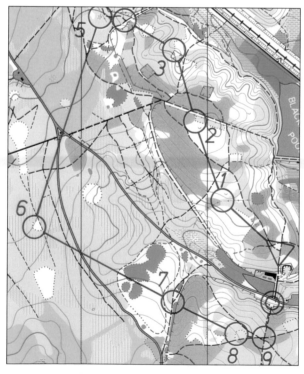

- these are skills to be learnt before progressing to the hard technical courses - green, blue and brown.

STRING COURSES

AGE GROUP
TIME

EQUIPMENT CHECKLIST

String courses are particularly good for giving under 8's the _feel_ of orienteering - running through trees, finding controls, punching a control card - almost an adventure.

The string is the means for laying a course for children to follow and not get lost. Controls should always be placed on very distinctive, preferably unique, features with the string following the easiest routes through the trees, across streams, even holes in thickets. Be creative but consider the leg length of a 3 year old!

Alternative string systems:

Finnish String Machine, 3km of nylon line with coloured flags.

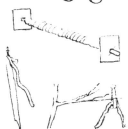

500 - 800 metres of orange baling twine or nylon line on cable drum of garden hose reel adapted with straps from old car safety belts.

String on wooden pole.

Light garden canes with fluorescent orange line attached or coloured plastic tape pegged to branches.

There are several ways of using a string course for beginners.

1 Premark a course on a simplified map. The string or tapes link up the controls. Follow the string, punch at each control as fast as you can.

2 Mark the line of the string on the map, 400 - 600 metres is long enough. Hang lots of controls (8-12) but only on unique features. Tie a coloured wax crayon to each control.

a) Children run round marking the card with the crayon at each control.

b) This time they mark the card and the map - identifying which feature they are beside ON THE LINE and marking the colour on the map to show where they are.

Simplified map for String course.

A child's map with colours marking positions of control points. For the very young String courses can also be used with picture maps to encourage or test map/ ground feature identification.

Control card with picture codes which will be found at each control.

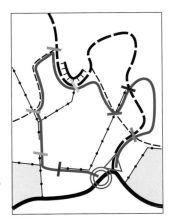

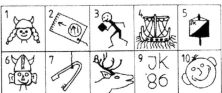

3 A white/yellow course could be surrounded by the string course used as a 'safety line' which must not be crossed but could be used for route choice.

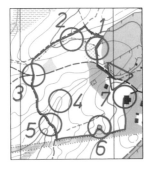

Children should be weaned onto selected white courses as soon as they can set the map and identify simple line features. These should build up confidence in making decisions and finding controls independently.

See also BOF Guidelines on String orienteering.

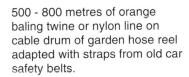

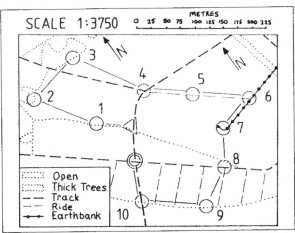

SCALE 1:3750   METRES   0 25 50 75 100 125 150 175 200 225

Open
Thick Trees
Track
Ride
Earthbank

COURSE PLANNING - FURTHER IDEAS

Courses in the play-ground/classroom

- Hang controls on distinctive features: a <u>corner</u> of a desk or building, not a side.

- Always use a template - the centre of the circle shows the control feature.

- Controls must be linked in a logical sequence.

- Hang or stick all controls at the same height.

Avoid 'dog legs' - they make the course unfair. Some will get an advantage from seeing others coming away from the control and will be <u>led</u> in.

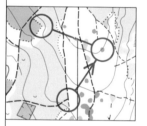
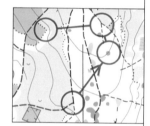

Competitors are most likely to go in and come out from the S. clearing by path.

A control is added to the North to lead orienteers out of the control a different way.

Create a white course from a Permanent Course.

The controls of a Permanent Course can be used by adding extra control sites to create a white course for beginners familiar with the area.

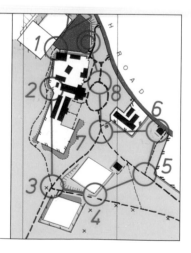

On a white course try using cards hanging from controls, rather than a sheet of lengthy instructions

Check that the code letters match your description list.	CAREFUL NOW! Follow the wall the right direction.	Set your map so that you can see which path to follow.	Can you see the next control?

Use taped routes to link controls in difficult terrain.

Controls 5, 6, 7 and 8 are linked by tapes on the ground. This is shown as a double line on the map and indicated in the control descriptions.

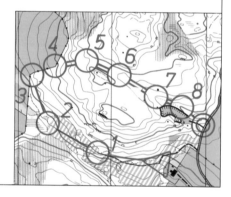

White course

- These courses are used by children who have never been on their own before.

- Don't be tempted to take them off the track.

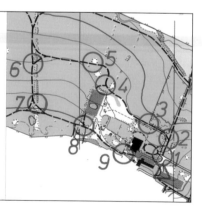

EVENT ORGANISATION 1

PREPARATION: PRE RACE DAY

* Register event with regional fixtures secretary for publicity and insurance. Appoint Controller to oversee arrangements.
* Seek permission and arrange access with landowners. Parking space influences start and finish.
* Publicise the event - posters, local press, radio.
* Collect and check equipment.
* Prizes, certificates, local sponsorship.
* Ask people to help and brief them well.
* Communicate with Controller from beginning.
* Process pre-entries when used.
* Invite local W.I. to sell drinks and food.
* Visit areas, plan courses, tape control sites. Code every control. Decide on Start and Finish sites.
* Draw master maps and get someone to check them.
* Type and copy control descriptions.
* Allocate punches to each control. Keep in polythene bags labelled with codes.
* Punch master course cards before putting out.
* Map corrections.
* Pre-mark maps for beginners courses.
* Ask the controller to check everything.
* Put out controls the day before if necessary - allow 15-20 minutes per kilometre to hang controls.

RACE DAY

REGISTRATION: in cars - tent - room
* To ease congestion keep cash/maps as a separate unit.
* Pre entry groups packs can be put together.
* One person looks after one course, and gives out:
    control descriptions
    control card
    start time

Registration officials' brief
* Offer a start time allowing time to get to the start (30 minutes).
* Write name on start list.
* Competing individuals from same group should start at least 5 minutes apart.
* Write in start time, full name/club on control card and stub.
* Every child should have a map even if competing as pair or in a family group.
* Direct to start and map corrections if necessary.

START
* Pre-start - calls time and takes stub, checking the time on the card.
* Start - blow whistle on each minute.
* Official at master maps to help beginners.

Starter's notes
* The start system must be watched carefully to make sure competitors start at the time on their card.
* They should be on the start line with one minute to go.
* Ensure that stubs are regularly transferred to results tent.

FINISH
A system for over 50 competitors with 4 people.
1 Calls "now" whenever anyone crosses the line.
2 Writes time on timesheet against each number in groups of 5 or 10.
3 Collects control cards in groups of 5 or 10 keeping them in order.
4 Keeps finishers in order.
or
1 Calls out time.
2 (and 3) Write times directly onto cards.

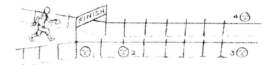

Finish notes
* A large tent or shed with tables and chairs makes the job easier for officials, especially in the rain.
* Numbered sticky labels can be put on cards as competitors finish.

RESULTS
1 Using time sheet, transfer times onto finisher's cards.
2 Calculate time taken - put onto course piles.
3 Check punch patterns (or colour) against master.
4 Transfer time taken to stub. Indicate if disqualified for missing or wrong controls.
5 Staple stubs to results strings - weather permitting.

Results notes
* The results team needs to be well organised under cover.
* A different coloured card for each course makes it much easier to check results.
* With large numbers 1 or 2 people per course is advisable. Stubs need to be brought from the start.

END OF RACE DAY
* Check that everyone has finished.
* Bring in controls if possible.

POST RACE DAY

* Produce a results list and post out as soon as possible.
* Thanks to landowners and helpers.
* Send results to local club secretary, local press.
* Pay debts and expenses, draw up financial statement.
* Collect all controls and tape (it may be possible to do this at the end of race day).
* Look at results - did everyone complete their course? Did you get the length right? Did you get the standard right?

Many informal low key events can be organised most satisfactorily with two or three people. Use the check lists to ensure you have thought of the essentials.

Create a 'do it yourself' registration with clear instructions with one person at the start and one at the finish. Ask participants to calculate their own time and staple the stub up.

Master maps could be copied and checked before the start.

Master control descriptions could also be copied on to the front or back of the control card.

GIVE YOURSELF PLENTY OF TIME TO GET EVERYTHING READY. AT LEAST TWO HOURS ARE NEEDED TO SET UP A COUPLE OF 1-2KM COURSES.

EVENT ORGANISATION 2

THE COURSES

- **Bright/fluorescent insulating tape** to identify control sites.
- **Control markers** and **codes** - include one for demonstration, 2 or 3 spare for replacement.
- **Punches** or crayons. Two or more may be needed at controls visited by more than one course (keep same pattern/colours).
- **Canes** and **string**. To hang markers/punches if nothing else is suitable.
- **Yellow tape** to mark off dangerous places.
- **Coloured tape** (not yellow) for taped routes and finish funnel.
- **String** for string courses.
- **Planners map** with all controls and codes.
  All courses, maps, descriptions and control flags should be double checked by a more experienced orienteer (the controller's role).
- **Master maps**
  - always draw with a stencil, 3-4 per course.
  - include descriptions.
  - seal in polythene bags.
  - tape onto boards.
  - attach red pens.
- **Pre-marked maps** for easiest courses - string course or under 10's.
- **Control descriptions** must be concise and describe the feature on the map. See rules book.

  Example:

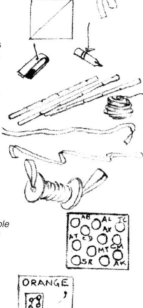

WHITE 1km 50m climb		
1	AB	Fence corner
2	TC	Path junction
3	CO	Gate
4	PL	Building N. corner
5	AT	Goal post
6	JR	Track bend
7	CM	Track junction

Navigate to finish - car park
Course closes 4.00pm

Capitals/lower4 case typing
Single spaces

Double space every 3 or 4 lines

Double space between numbers codes and descriptions

- **Master control cards** for each course marked with correct pattern or colour.
- **SLOW! Runners crossing**. Signs for any road crossing.

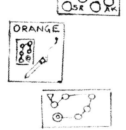

PARKING AND ASSEMBLY

- **Signposting** to the event and at the event (how far to the start? etc.).
- **Toilet facilities** - rolls, pits, cover etc.
- **Litter bags**

REGISTRATION

- **Maps** (if not pre-marked).
- **Control cards** for each course.
- **Control descriptions** for each course.
- **Cash box** (and **float**).
- **Start lists** for start times + clipboards.
- **Notices** - what courses are on offer Course notice for each car or table.
- **Map corrections**. 3-5 copies clearly labelled. Number each correction. Make sure everyone sees them.
- Large supply of **safety pins** and **polythene bags** to help beginners get organised.

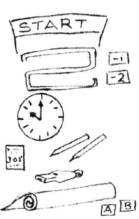

START

- **Start banner**
- **Tape** to separate starting lanes and to lead to master maps.
- **Pre-start** and -1 and -2 countdown notices (waterproof).
- **Box** for stubs.
- **Large clock** to show 'race time'. plus 1 - 2 watches synchronised with Finish.
- **Spare stubs** for each course in case anyone forgets.
- **Waterproof pens** and pencils for notes or extra instructions.
- **Gong** or whistle to start.
- **Protection** for master maps if wet.
- **Course labels** for master maps.

FINISH

- **Finish banner**
- **Tape** (and posts) leading from last control and funnelling competitors into the finish.
- **Clock** and synchronised watches.
- **Paper** for time sheets, numbered in 5's or 10's.
- **Spirit based** or **wax pens** for writing on wet cards.
- **Rubber bands** to keep cards and time sheets together.
- **Spare cards** to replace lost ones.
- **Orange squash**, cups, water.
- **Litter bags**.
- **First aid** and qualified administrator.
- **String/cord** for results. Staples.
- **Prizes**?
- **Local club information**. Next events etc.
- **Envelopes** for posting results.

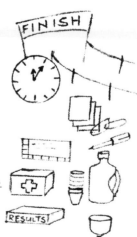

SAFETY AND RULES

For Competitors

Always report to the finish whether you have finished the course or not - otherwise someone will search for you.

Competitors take part entirely at their own risk.

A whistle should always be carried - only to be used in an emergency. 6 long whistle blasts repeated after a pause:

— — — — — —

3 short blasts will be made in reply when someone comes to search for you:

- - -

Carry a compass in unknown terrain and know how to follow a safety bearing.

A watch is recommended for group departure and course closure times.

Body and full leg cover must be worn. Sleeveless shirts are allowed. A windproof jacket is recommended in wet, windy conditions.

Ensure that you are fit enough to run the course and are not recovering from a cold or feeling off colour. If in doubt do not compete.

Select a course which you can complete.

Competitors should orienteer independently unless they have entered as a pair or group. There should be no following or seeking information from other competitors.

The Country Code must always be followed:-

- Take your litter home.

- Stiles and gates should be used when they are marked as crossing points on the map.

- Running across gardens or fields planted with crops is forbidden.

Never enter areas marked out of bounds on the map.

In point to point orienteering, controls must be visited in the correct order. Any control missed incurs disqualification.

For Leaders:

Decide whether children can run/compete in pairs.

Assess the risks - are there any areas you do not want children to enter.

Ensure that each child has a parental consent form.

Carry a first aid box when taking a group to an event.

Make sure your group knows the safety bearing to be followed if completely lost.

Shouting and calling are to be discouraged.

Beginners should be encouraged to move away from control points to plan their next route so that they do not draw attention to the control.

Inform the organiser when all the group has returned.

13

MAPMAKING

Mapping is a task that many people feel they are unable to tackle. However it is relatively easy to produce a simple, useful school map at a fairly low cost. This chapter explains how this is done and gives lists of recommended symbols.

Mapping is an activity that a group/class can be involved with - fieldwork, computer drawing, map design.

Making a map can be a valuable project for an interested individual

FIELDWORK FOR A SCHOOL MAP

Base map

The first stage in producing a simple orienteering map is usually to find an existing map to use as a base. If the intention is to make a map of a school, the architects' plans may be the best material - there is usually an overall site plan at a scale suitable for an orienteering map (1:1000-1:2500).

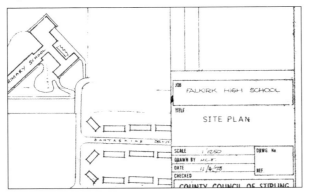

When making a map of a park or woodland, an official map is usually the only accurate material available. These maps are published at various scales. In the UK there are 1:2500 maps of urban areas. The OS 1:10000 map is rather small scale for this kind of map but this is the largest OS scale that includes contour information.

If the base material is not at the scale you wish to use, enlargement or reduction is most cheaply done on a photocopier.

Remember that to copy any map, permission must be obtained from the copyright holder (who may make a charge).

Survey

The next stage is to take the base map and make any changes required. This involves adding new detail and reclassifying features already on the map to an orienteering specification. Exactly what to include on a map will vary from area to area. A look at similar maps is the best guide to what is needed.

Two skills are needed - using a protractor compass and pace counting. The positioning of new detail is done either with a compass (for direction) or pacing (for distance), or a combination of both. In a school environment all new detail can often be plotted simply

by taking distance measurements, without getting involved with compass bearings. You will need to practise a metre pace length or know how to convert your normal pacing.

To plot a line accurately using a compass the base map must have magnetic north lines for reference. Magnetic north is best worked out as follows (north arrows on architects' plans are often inaccurate):

- Take a bearing (b) along an existing straight line on the map (edge of building or road).
- Set an angle of (360 - b)° on the compass.
- Rotate the whole compass until the lines on the base of the housing are parallel with the line of the feature on the map.
- A line now drawn along the edge of the base plate will be the real magnetic north

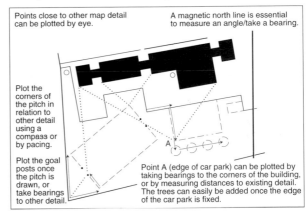

A combination of plotting angles and measuring distances will allow you to fix the position of any objects in the area. Anything which is distinct on the ground can be shown on a simple orienteering map. Be careful not to include too much detail or the map will be difficult to read.

Look at the symbol lists that follow to see how features on the ground should be classified to make your map an orienteering map.

It is good practice to produce a clean copy of all the detail to be included on the map. This is best done by putting an overlay over the base map and (a) tracing the existing detail to be retained and (b) adding new detail that has been surveyed. A polyester drawing film is the best material for the overlay.

If this draft is drawn carefully it can be used as the master for photocopying without any further work.

COPIES OF A COLOUR MAP

There are a number of options for transforming the results of field work into maps ready for use.

PHOTOCOPYING/HAND COLOURING

A well drawn survey draft can be copied and used in black and white, or hand coloured - see mapping exercise p32.

Alternatively the original draft could be hand coloured if there is access to a colour copier.

HAND DRAWING

Traditional artwork for a colour map involved hand drawing separate overlays for each colour. This is still an option but the advent of computers in schools has overtaken this method (see below).

Lines are drawn with special drawing pens with different nibs giving different line thicknesses. Point symbols are either drawn with a pen or applied from dry transfer (rub-on) sheets. Areas/patterns are applied by cutting shapes from sheets of self adhesive film. Materials are available from specialist orienteering mapmaking suppliers (see also *Mapmaking for Orienteers* reference at the end of this book).

COMPUTER DRAWING

If the teacher or the class has access to a computer with suitable software the map could be drawn as part of the classroom activities. A simple drawing programme is all that is needed for a school map. The drawing programme must be able to do a number of things:

- draw a line and colour it. The possibility of drawing curved lines is preferable but a curved line can be a series of short straight lines if necessary.
  - draw shapes and colour them.
  - change the orientation of lines and objects.

Even simple drawing programmes can usually do much more than this. After a short time the children will probably be more expert than the teacher!

There is an orienteering map drawing programme called OCAD. This is relatively inexpensive and widely used throughout the orienteering world.

The first step is to get the information from the draft map on the computer. There are options depending on the availability of equipment:

- to scan the draft and have it on screen as a template to trace over.
- to use a digitising tablet.
- to transfer information by eye/measurement - a grid drawn on the draft and on the screen is the starting stage.

MAP LAYOUT

The design of a map should include various items of information:

- the map itself
- title, and logos if required
- scale, scale bar, (contour interval if relevant)
- key to all the symbols used
- magnetic north lines
- credits to copyright owners, disclaimers, etc.

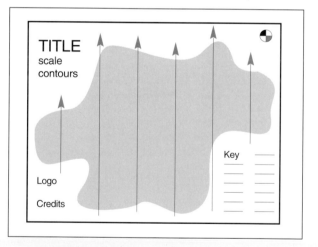

REPRODUCTION

Once the map is drawn it is relatively cheap to run off colour copies as required. With a map drawn on computer amendments can be made very quickly and new copies produced. Colour copies can be mounted or heatsealed for repeated use.

If a large number of copies is required, commercial colour printing of a map will be cheaper than colour laserprinting. It also gives a higher quality of print. Consultation with a printer or mapmaking company such as Harveys at the outset is essential if problems are to be avoided, particularly if hand drawing.

A good computer drawing programme will handle this aspect of the process automatically.

MAP SYMBOLS

It is advisable to keep to standard orienteering map symbols as tar as possible as this reduces confusion. The symbols for a 5 colour map (right) are an international standard.

SINGLE COLOUR SCHOOL MAP

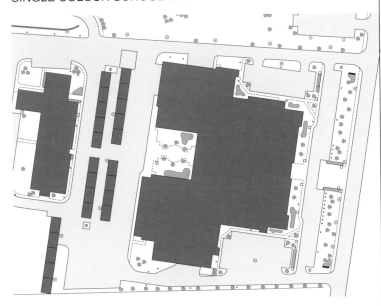

THREE COLOUR SCHOOL MAP

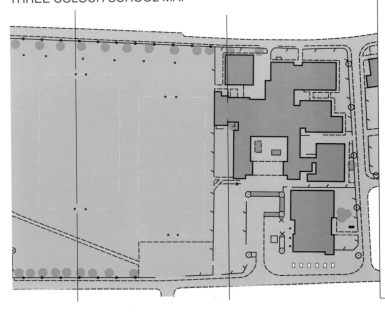

	open land
	rough open land
	felled area
	forest: run
	forest: slow run
	forest: walk
	forest: impenetrable
	distinct vegetation change
	major road
	minor road
	dirt road
	vehicle track
	large path
	small path
	narrow ride
	wide ride
	fence
	uncrossable fence
	power line
	impassable cliff
	contour
	index contour
	form line
	knoll : large small
	depression : large small
	pit
	dry ditch
	steep bank
	platform
	gully
	earth bank
	pond
	crossable wide stream
	crossable stream
	ditch
	uncrossable marsh
	marsh
	open marsh
	spring
	water tank
	building
	ruin
	trig. pillar
	grave
	firing range
	shaft
	car parking area
	shooting platform

PICTURE MAPS

A picture map is simply an oblique view of the area from above. It is relatively simple to draw using a map as the base.

Picture maps are useful for very young children as a first step towards using a map. However do not spend too long using these maps or the step to real maps will be quite difficult.

The difficulty in using a picture map is that it views the area from one particular point. The further the child moves from that point, the less useful the 'picture' becomes.

The examples should give some ideas.

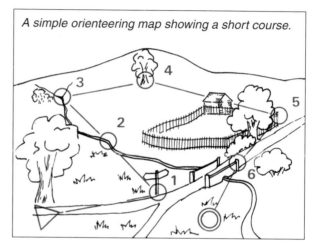

A simple orienteering map showing a short course.

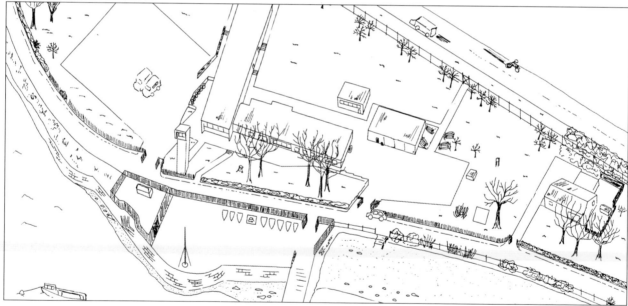

Even a single school building and playground can be used for a picture map.

14

ORIENTEERING FOR PEOPLE WITH DISABILITIES

The opportunity for people with both learning and physical disabilities to participate in orienteering activities has seen rapid development in recent years.

The goal is for full integration making the sport open to all. Realistically the nature of the sport, especially the rough terrain that competitors often compete in, limits opportunities for wheelchair users on standard courses. However, some of the major events on the orienteering fixture list are now offering a form of the sport 'trail orienteering' that provides an answer.

This section offers guidelines for trail orienteering and suggestions for introducing and developing map skills for people with learning difficulties.

TRAIL ORIENTEERING

AIM
* *to provide competitive orienteering for people of all abilities*

Trail orienteering is orienteering on untimed courses where the challenges to the participant are mental (not physical) and achievement is based upon the ability to interpret the map and its relationship to the ground. This makes it possible for people with disabilities to participate.

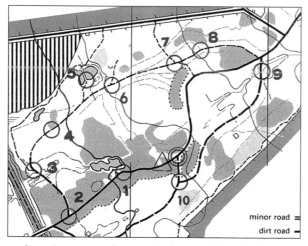

A novice course (one control at each location)

Competitors stay on paths (which must be navigable by wheelchairs). Competitors can walk, propel themselves, be pushed or use power driven chairs.

Once beyond the novice stage they gain points for making correct decisions in a multi-choice situation.

At a predetermined viewing point the competitor can see a number of control markers. One of the markers corresponds precisely to the control on the competitor's map. Competitors punch the relevant box on the control card to indicate their choice (A, B or C). The number of options increases with course difficulty

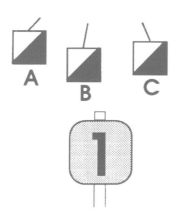

Maps are usually pre-printed with a course.

The control description sheet may have written descriptions or I.O.F. pictorial ones.

Each competitor is issued with a punch. A card at the viewing or decision making point identifies the control number.

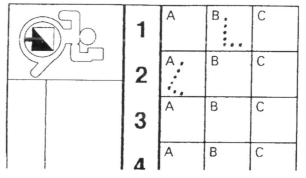

CONTROL CARD (correct box to be punched at each control)

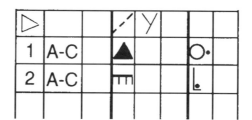

IOF PICTORIAL CONTROL DESCRIPTIONS

Trail orienteering technical guidelines

Class	N	C	B	A	E
Colour	CREAM	ROSE	SKY	FAWN	GREY
Terrain	Easy. Not steep. No small paths. Open areas/buildings used.	As N	More woodland terrain. Gradients. Small paths can be used.	Mostly woodland terrain. Hills used. Small paths used a lot.	As A
Map	Not too many details. No use of contours.	As N	Varied maps, with more detail in parts. Easy contours used.	As varied as possible. Contour lines very important.	As A
Degree of difficulty	No route choice. Few changes of direction. From 0-2 junctions. No crossovers.	As N	Simple route choice. Variety of leg length. Many changes of direction. Dog legs. Crossovers avoided.	Complicated route choice to controls. Large variation in paths used. Many dog legs used.	As A
Use of compass	To orientate map only.	N-S, E-W only	1 compass problem, e.g. N. side of feature.	2 or more problems, e.g. N. one of group on S. side.	As A, perhaps looking from E.
Control points	Very easy, on or close to line. Precise control descriptions.	As N	Line features and large point feature. Simple control description.	Small features. Knowledge of contours. Difficult descriptions.	As A. Smaller and less obvious details if possible.
False control	None	Very different feature	Not on similar feature.	Parallel/similar feature desirable. False site not necessarily on map	As A. All markers may be on false sites.
No. of markers at site	1	2	3	4	5
Attack point	Only distant line features.	As N	Line features. Some obvious point and contour features.	Small features including contour lines.	As A, but can be further from control.
Viewing point	Yes (+ punch)	Yes	Yes	Yes	Yes
Length	1-2km	As N	1.5-2.5km	1.5-3km	1.5-3.5km
No. of controls	8-10	10-12	12-15	15-20	15-25
Distance from path to control site	0-5m	0-10m	0-20m	0-40m	0-40m+
Timed controls	No	No	1 (2?)	minimum 1	minimum 2

Competitors may move up and down the path to view the array of control markers. The marker farthest to the left when viewed from the marked decision point is deemed to be A and those to the right of it B, C etc. Competitors simply indicate by punching the correct box on the control card which marker they think accords with the centre of the circle on their map.

In conventional competition timing to the nearest second establishes the finishing order. With Trail Orienteering completing the course is not timed but because at the end of the event a number of competitors could have the same score, a 'tie break' method has been established. At one or two control sites the time used in decision making is taken.

Controls should be on definite features (fence corner, etc.). There must be one right answer. In elite competition contour features are frequently used but they should be avoided for beginners.

Adaptations

(i) line events, where control markers are placed on a line or near to it and points are scored for punching the control card box when a marker is on the line and for leaving blanks when it isn't.

(ii) team competition where the scores of a predetermined number of competitors are combined.

Further work

Refer to Trail Orienteering published by Harveys 1994.

Trail Orienteering (p15): using table top picture maps.

Trail Orienteering (p16, 17): treasure island.

Trail Orienteering (p18, 19): star exercise.

MAP SKILLS FOR PEOPLE WITH LEARNING DIFFICULTIES

AIM
• to provide worthwhile learning experiences and a form of competitive orienteering for people with mild or moderate learning difficulties

The demands of map reading and decision making whilst under time pressure are central to the sport and an attraction to its followers. Reading complex maps in particular might be expected to be beyond children or adults who have learning difficulties. Recent experimental work has shown however that, if the emphasis is on the sequence of activities designed to introduce and develop techniques and not on the learning difficulties of the beginners, then it is possible for children or adults with mild learning difficulties to gain sufficient expertise to complete colour coded courses.

A programme should be designed that includes:

• establishing trust and confidence with the learners

• introducing the concept that plans and maps are patterns of shapes (p20)

• simple map making using desks, the classroom and the gymnasium (p19)

• teaching map symbols and scale (p19)

• setting/orientating the map (p26)

• using the map for map walks, streamer courses, string and off string courses (p24)

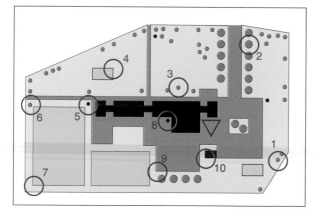

It is advisable to introduce new concepts slowly and to commence each lesson by revising what has been practised in previous sessions.

Success is more likely if
• the class size is small - teacher/pupil ratio of 1:4.
• the pace of the lesson is slow with much repetition.
• activities are always from the simple to the complex.
• all lessons are basically practical using a variety of learning resources.
• beginners progress at their own pace rather than at that of the group.

• much positive feedback and encouragement is given.
• there is a sense of success and enjoyment within each lesson.
• beginners are not put into a situation which will lead to a sense of failure.

It is particularly important that maps used are clear and uncluttered. It is an advantage if the groups are familiar with the area being used and that they follow the sequence of

• map walk,
• following streamers to identify control sites,
• string courses,
• basic very easy point to point courses with controls on line features.

It may be many weeks before the beginners feel confident enough to tackle a white colour-coded course and initially the early attempts might be best attempted in pairs.

Appendix 1   BOF FIXTURES STRUCTURE

Scandinavians call orienteering the forest sport. The International Orienteering Federation rules discuss suitable terrain in terms of detailed forested areas with limited visibility, sparse track networks and numerous small features. Britain does not present the most promising scene for a navigational sport developed in the vast forested wilderness of Northern Europe.

It is not surprising therefore that the first tentative steps in introducing orienteering to Britain should have happened in Scotland in the early 1960's, nor that early developments in England centred around the South Ribble club in the Pennines. However a powerful push in the early days of the mid 1960's came from the commons, military training areas and the suburban parks of Surrey. It was in Richmond that the English Orienteering Association was born and right from the early days British Orienteering developed its own imaginative philosophy in exploiting the navigational potential of country parks, open moorland, village commons, the complicated road networks of housing estates and reclaimed industrial sites.

The British Orienteering Federation's fixture structure reflects the diversity of terrain and the necessity to preserve prime areas and to use their potential in an economical and imaginative manner. Small patches of woodland are linked with open areas to provide local events and night orienteering. Planted forests with grid patterns of paths are used for introductory events. British course planning has to be inventive and flexible in order to make the best use of limited areas.

The present fixtures structure grew out of the findings

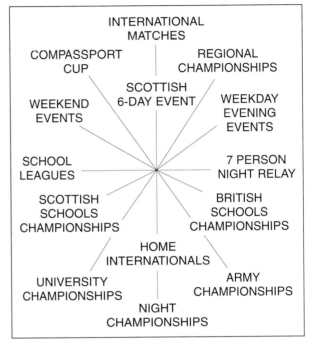

of a working party set up in 1983 which recommended four layers of fixtures each with its own standards.

The UK has a British Schools Orienteering Association which promotes good practice and relevant major schools competitions

A wide variety of events exists inside and outside the competition structure.

BRITISH CHAMPIONSHIPS • JAN KJELLSTROM EASTER 2-DAY EVENT

Age groups 10-70, plus elite classes.

This fixtures structure is currently (1997) under review.

NATIONAL EVENTS (12 per year, spread through regions)

Age group 10-70, plus elite classes. Entry must be made in advance. Colour coded courses often available.

'BADGE' EVENTS

Age group 10-70, plus elite. Pre-entry or entry on the day. National Badge Award Scheme. Colour coded courses often available.

OPEN / CLUB EVENTS (including introductory events).

Courses usually colour coded, open to individuals or pairs
White - yellow - orange - red - green - blue - brown (string course often available for the under 10's).

Appendix 2 PERSONAL PERFORMANCE

The Personal Performance Ladder

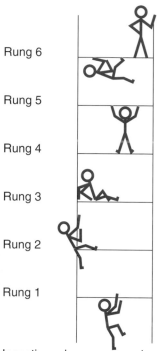

Rung 6

THE TOP: World Championships
Strengths and weaknesses • psychological factors • peaking and periodisation

Rung 5

GETTING THERE: National Squad, international training camps/competition
Orienteering strategies • balance of speed and certainty

Rung 4

AIMING HIGH: Regional Squad
Compass and pacing - relocation • refinement of techniques • a year plan

Rung 3

NATIONAL BADGE: National & Badge events, Championships
Contours, route choice • planned physical and technical training • working hard at club coaching sessions

Rung 2

COLLECTING COLOURS: Colour Coded Events
Use of handrails • simple route choice • introduction to the compass • helped by club coaching

Rung 1

GETTING STARTED: Club, School, Outdoor Centre
Understanding the map as a picture • orientating the map to the ground

Incentive schemes are an important part of the sport and exist at different levels. A national ranking system for senior age classes is based on results in Badge and National events. After a hesitant start the colour coded system has succeeded in providing competition of graded technical and physical difficulty with cheap on-the-day entry. Awards are available for successfully completing a number of colour coded courses.

The National Badge Scheme awards iron, bronze, silver, gold and championships badges after three events have been completed within a time based on the average of the first three in each class, e.g. gold - average of the first three plus 25%; silver - average plus 50%, etc.

The Scottish Orienteering Association has long run a scheme where '5', '10' and '20' badges can be gained after completing the appropriate number of timed events. This has proved an excellent scheme for beginners.

A full fixture list and details of incentive schemes is published in each issue of the national magazine 'Compass Sport'.

Competitions and incentive schemes are designed to provide the motivation for individuals to improve their orienteering techniques and overall personal competence. The figure above shows a personal performance ladder and indicates the route to the top for the ambitious orienteer.

Supporting the growth and development of personal competence is a National and Junior Squad structure and a comprehensive coaching scheme.

The Senior Squad aims directly at preparation for World Championships. With the help of Sports Council funds it provides a programme of home and overseas courses and competitions tailored to the short and long term plans of individual members, each of whom has a personal coach.

The Junior Squad seeks to identify outstanding young orienteers in Britain and to develop their technical ability so as to provide a foundation of good orienteers upon which Britain's international programme can be built. Home competition programmes and overseas links and training camps have produced a dramatic improvement in the performance of our junior teams.

Regional Squads cater for juniors with potential who wish to develop their skills and physical fitness. These squads, catering for the 13-17 age groups, organise weekend courses and in some cases overseas training.

Appendix 3

NATIONAL SENIOR SQUAD (20)	Chairman Coach Assistant Coaches	Objective: World Championship performance
NATIONAL JUNIOR SQUAD (35-50) 16-25 years	Chairman Coach (under 21 group) Coach (induction courses)	Objective: Development of junior elite potential
12 REGIONAL JUNIOR SQUADS	Regional Co-ordinator Assistant Coaches	Objective: Development of junior standards
CLUB/SCHOOL COACHING STRUCTURES		Objective: Enhancement of technical and physical performance at all levels

RECOMMENDED TIMES (1997) at National events

CLASS	WINNING TIME	TECHNICAL DIFFICULTY	CLASS	WINNING TIME	TECHNICAL DIFFICULTY
M10	20-25	2	W10	20-25	2
M12	25-35	3	W12	25-35	3
M14	35-45	3/4	W14	30-40	3/4
M16	50-60	5	W16	40-50	5
M18	60-70	5	W18	50-60	5
M20	70-80	5	W20	60-70	5
M21E	90-100	5	W21E	65-75	5
M21A	80-90	5	W21A	65-75	5
M35	70-80	5	W35	60-70	5
M40	65-75	5	W40	60-70	5
M45	60-70	5	W45	55-65	5
M50	60-70	5	W50	55-65	5
M55	60-70	5	W55	55-65	5
M60	55-65	5	W60	55-65	5
M65	55-65	5	W65	55-65	5
M70	55-65	5	W70	55-65	5
M75	55-65	5	W75	55-65	5

Note: Age class applies from 1st January each year, e.g. if a boy has his 16th birthday on 10th August he enters M16 from 1st January of that year.

Elite (E) class - at National events only.

Juniors are offered A and B courses where the B course is technically easier and shorter. Seniors (M/W20+) have the choice of long or short courses in each age group at the same technical level.

Colour coded courses (p132) may be offered at National and Badge events to cater for newcomers and recreational orienteers. Similarly novice or string courses may be provided.

GUIDE TO TECHNICAL LEVELS

LEVEL 1

Technical

- controls on line features, usually paths
- controls close together, at every decision point
- no route choice
- routes follow line features (tracks and paths

LEVEL 3 (level 2 between 1 and 3)

Technical

- controls on easier point features
- controls near obvious attack points
- 'catching' line features behind controls
- some route choice but good navigating features
- quickest routes go direct but easier and longer alternatives available
- encourage simple use of contour detail

LEVEL 5 (level 4 between 3 and 5)

Technical

- controls on any features but not hidden
- controls far from collecting features but enough detail in control areas for accurate navigation
- errors at controls expensive
- as few controls as necessary for good planning
- legs demanding a range of techniques

Appendix 4 BOF COACHING STRUCTURE

The BOF Coaching Structure

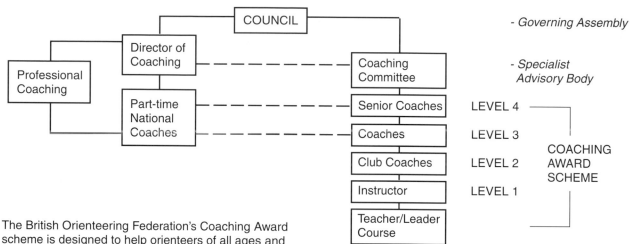

The British Orienteering Federation's Coaching Award scheme is designed to help orienteers of all ages and levels of ability to realise their full potential through a uniform system of instruction and thereby enhance their enjoyment of the sport. The scheme is divided into three levels with dual qualification at the basic level.

The initial entry to coaching is the teacher/leader certificate which is aimed at beginner teachers/instructors and is gained by attendance at a two day course. It is not examined.

LEVEL 1

Instructor: the award is aimed at teachers, youth leaders, outdoor activity instructors and any others involved in introducing orienteering mainly to young people.

Club Coach: to work with beginners and less experienced orienteers of all ages at club level.

LEVEL 2

Coach: to be involved with personal performance at regional and national level, training and assessing candidates for level 1 awards.

LEVEL 3

Senior Coach. The holder is an expert in orienteering who may have responsibility for a specific area of coaching at National level. He/she contributes to the running of courses, National Squad coaching, the development of coaching techniques and the generation and dissemination of coaching ideas.

Full qualification and assessment conditions for each level of award can be obtained from the BOF National Office. Detailed information on coaching, physical training and techniques is contained in the BOF's Training and Coaching Manual. The BOF's coaching activities are co-ordinated by a full-time Director of Coaching, who has responsibility for part-time National Coaches who fill specific posts within the scheme.

Appendix 5   ORIENTEERING IN THE USA

Orienteering in the United States is thought to have begun in 1946, when Björn Kjellstrom, a champion orienteer and skier from Sweden, promoted map making and holding meets. The first meet was held in Dunes Park by Lake Michigan and was set up for Boy Scouts.

The first public meet in the United States was held in the Valley Forge National Park and this led to the foundation of the oldest club in the country, Delaware Valley. The sport has spread slowly through the 1980s and 90s and, at present, 65 clubs located in most states organize events for about 10,000 regular competitors.

The United States' orienteering schedule of events is organized across eight regions that cover the continent from the northeast region, which includes New England, New York and northern New Jersey, to the Pacific region, which covers California, Arizona, Nevada, Utah and Hawaii.

Each club in the United States reports active mapping of new areas, the ability to host local and national meets, and terrain worthy of a visit. The success of orienteering festivals and multi-events over the past few years should ensure that the sport continues to expand in the United States during the years ahead.

Because of the great distances between orienteering centers in the United States, opportunities are limited for orienteers across the continent to meet and discuss their sport. The United States Orienteering Federations' (USOF) annual convention, an event unique to America, may be the answer. The convention includes four days of workshops, clinics, working parties and discussion groups - in addition to the orienteering competitions.

Addresses:

United States Orienteering Federation
PO Box 1444
Forest Park, GA 30051
1-404-363-2110 (tel. & fax)

Magazine:
Orienteering North America
SM & L Berman Publishing Co.
23 Fayette Street
Cambridge, MA 02139
1-617-868-7416

USOF Clubs by Region

Northeast
Western Connecticut OC
New England OC
Cambridge Sports Union
Hudson Valley O
Empire OC
Buffalo OC
Rochester OC
Central NY O
Long Island OC
Adirondack OK
US Military Academy OC
Orienteering Unlimited
   OC
Wilderness Orienteering
   Camps
Green Mountain OC

Mid-Atlantic
Delaware Valley O
Assoc
Indiana Univ. of Penn.
Susquehanna Valley O
Land of the Vikings OC
Pocono OC
Warrior Ridge OC
Quantico OC
Fork Union Military
   Academy OC

Southeast
Vulcan OC
Florida Orienteering
Georgia OC
Blue Star Complex
Backwoods OK
Triad OC
Carolina OK
Tennessee OC

Heartland
Rocky Mountain OC
Chicago Area OC
Iowa OC
Orienteer Kansas
Minnesota OC
St Louis OC
Possum Trot OC
N Dakota O Alliance
Badger OC

OC/K = Orienteering Club

Mid-West
O Louisville
Southern Michigan OC
North Eastern Ohio OC
O Club of Cincinnati
Miami Valley OC
Central Ohio OC

Southwest
Ark-La-Tex O Society
Sooner OC
Houston OC
North Texas O Association
Hill Country OC
Aggie Pathfinders

Pacific
Tucson OC
Phoenix OC
Bay Area OC
Los Angeles OC
San Diego Orienteering
Gold Country Orienteers

Northwest
Arctic OC
Columbia River OC
Jefferson State OC
Cascade OC
Chuckanut Orienteers
Eastern Washington OC
Ellensburg OC
Husky OC
Nisqually O
Sacajawea Orienteers
Sammamish OC

Appendix 6 REFERENCES / SOURCES

BOOKS

Orienteering
> Tom Renfrew, *Human Kinetics 1996*

Orienteering in the National Curriculum (Eng/Wales) Key Stages 1+2
> McNeill, Martland, Palmer, *Harveys 1992*

Orienteering in the National Curriculum (Eng/Wales) Key Stages 3+4
> McNeill, Palmer, *Harveys 1993*

Orienteering in the Scottish 5-14 Curriculum
> Renfrew, Michie, *Harveys 1994*

Orienteering for the Young
> *International Orienteering Federation*

Pathways to Excellence
> Peter Palmer, *Harveys 1994*

Principles of Course Planning
> *International Orienteering Federation*

Rules and Guidelines.
> *British Orienteering Federation*

Skills of the Game
> Carol McNeill, *Crowood Press 1996*

Start Orienteering (series of 5 books)
> Carol McNeill, Tom Renfrew, *Harveys*

Trail Orienteering
> Anne Braggins, *Harveys 1993*

MAGAZINES

Compass Sport (UK). Eight issues per annum.
> Subscriptions: 37 Sandicoombe Road, Twickenham, Middlesex, TW1 2LR

Handrail (UK). Four issues per annum.
> Subscriptions: 28 Merrifield Road, Ford, nr. Salisbury, Wiltshire, SP4 6DF

Orienteering North America (USA)
> SM & L Berman Publishing Co.
> 23 Fayette Street
> Cambridge, MA 02139

VIDEOS

Orienteering - the first steps

Orienteering - Going for it

Challenge to Sport - Orienteering

Orienteering Skills (5 parts)

All books and videos available from Harveys

BRITISH ORIENTEERING FEDERATION (BOF)

'Riversdale' Dale Road North, Darley Dale, Matlock, Derbyshire DE4 2HS.
Telephone: 0629 734042 (answerphone service)

Information available on membership, clubs, permanent orienteering and wayfaring courses, coaching awards, schools schemes and fixtures.

Introductory packs for individuals, clubs and schools are part of a 'dispatch by return' service.

HARVEYS

12-16 Main Street, Doune, Perthshire, FK16 6BJ
Telephone: 01786 841202. Fax: 01786 841098

Orienteering equipment, books, videos, starter packs for teaching orienteering.

A complete mapmaking service - base maps, survey, cartography, printing

Catalogue available on request

UNITED STATES ORIENTEERING FEDERATION (USOF)

PO Box 1444
Forest Park, GA 30051
1-404-363-2110 (tel. & fax)

HUMAN KINETICS

PO Box 5076, Champaign, IL 61825-5076, USA

Appendix 7   GLOSSARY

Aiming off - a technique involving deliberately aiming to one side of a point on a linear feature, so there is only one way to turn to find the control.

Attack point - a large feature close to a control used in the selection and execution of a route.

Bearing - the direction you want to travel.

BOF - British Orienteering Federation.

Collecting feature - a long feature used as a point of reference when following a route or to keep you from running too far beyond a control.

Colour-coded courses - a series of courses (white, yellow, orange, red, green, blue, brown) where each colour has a standard degree of technical and physical difficulty. Colours vary from country to country.

Contours - lines on the map joining points of equal height, from which ground shapes and steepness can be judged.

Control - various terms are used - point, marker, kite.

Control card - carried to mark/punch each control visited.

Control code - identification letters/numbers displayed at the control site and included on the description list.

Control descriptions - a list of precise descriptions of the control sites, either written or as symbols.

Control flow - the ease/efficiency with which a competitor passes through a control site, checking the code, punching the card, deciding the exit route from the control, in the minimum time.

Course - the sequence of control points marked on a map which have to be visited in the correct order.

Dog-leg - a poorly planned leg that allows orienteers to be led into a control by seeing others leaving and thus gaining an advantage.

Event - an organised competition for orienteers (also called a **Meet**).

Form line - an intermediate or auxiliary contour line.

Fine orienteering - precise navigation, maintaining contact with the map throughout.

Fight - a term used to describe vegetation which reduces running speed to 20-50% (shown as dark green on the map).

Handrail - a line feature that can be used to aid navigation and simplify map reading.

Leg - the section of a course between two controls.

Legend (or key) - a list of the symbols on the map.

M - male classes, e.g. M13 (boys aged 13-14).

Master map - used to copy a course on to a map.

Magnetic north lines - shown on all orienteering maps to avoid the necessity of adjusting a bearing for declination.

Orientating a map (orienting in USA, Canada and Australia) - turning the map until North on the map points to North in the terrain.

Pace counting - counting double paces to measure distance covered on the ground.

Pre-marked maps - no master maps, the map is given at the start line with the course already marked.

Pre-start - your call up time, 1-3 minutes before your start time.

Re-entrant - a small valley shown by one or more contour lines.

Relocation - finding yourself when lost.

Ride - a firebreak or grassy break between lines of trees.

Rough orienteering - running quickly taking note of only the major features along the route.

Score orienteering - a form of the sport in which competitors have a set period of time to visit as many controls as possible, in any order. Each control has a points value according to difficulty and distance.

Setting - orientating (orienting) the map.

Stub - the part of the control card which is handed in at the pre-start; also used to show results.

Thumbing - holding the map folded with your thumb beside your location.

Transpaseal - trade name for self adhesive covering used to protect the map.

Vegetation change - the boundary between two distinct types of vegetation, e.g. white (runnable forest) and green (slow run forest). A very distinct boundary will be shown by a dotted black line.

W - female classes, e.g. W15 (girls aged 15 and 16).

Walk - a term used to describe vegetation which reduces running speed to 50-80% (shown as mid green on the map).